101 WAYS
TO PROTECT YOUR JOB

BOOKS BY GEORGE DE MARE

THE EMPIRE (novel)

THE RULING PASSION (novel)

COMMUNICATING AT THE TOP

CORPORATE LIVES (*with Joanne Summerfield*)

LISTENING—It Can Change Your Life
(*co-author with Dr. Lyman K. Steil and Joanne Summerfield*)

101 Ways to Protect Your Job

*A handbook on how to handle your most
valuable single asset, your job.
Advice from experts.*

GEORGE DE MARE

with Joanne Summerfield

McGRAW-HILL BOOK COMPANY

*New York   St. Louis   San Francisco   Auckland   Bogotá   Guatemala
Hamburg   Johannesburg   Lisbon   London   Madrid   Mexico
Montreal   New Delhi   Panama   Paris   San Juan   São Paulo
Singapore   Sydney   Tokyo   Toronto*

1 2 3 4 5 6 7 8 9 D O C D O C 8 7 6 5 4 3

ISBN 0-07-016289-1 {H.C.}
       0-07-016285-9 {PBK.}

Library of Congress Cataloging in Publication Data

De Mare, George.
    101 ways to protect your job.
    1. Job security. 2. Success. 3. Job hunting.
I. Summerfield, Joanne. II. Title. III. Title:
One hundred one ways to protect your job. IV. Title:
One hundred and one ways to protect your job.
HD5708.4.D4 1984   650.1   83-11340
ISBN 0-07-016289-1
ISBN 0-07-016285-9 (pbk.)

Book design by Chris Simon

CONTENTS

This book tells you:

How you can tell whether you are competent.
What four measurements are usually used in the work world to help you measure yourself.
What you should know about relating to your boss.
What four psychological types are found in modern organizations.
What are the worst jobs.
What you should know about meeting deadlines.
Eight ways the bureaucracy can kill new ideas.
What principles of persuasion have been found effective.
Four approaches used to get out from under a bad boss.
Three ways someone in the organization can "get" you and what to do about them.
The importance of a mentor.
Nine reasons why you may not be liked.
What happens when you are in the "wrong" company for you.
When you should be frank and when you shouldn't.
The three basic levels of communicating and the seven basic forms of communicating in an organization.

The importance of listening and the four areas where listening failure may occur.

The importance of the grapevine and four steps to take to plug into it.

When you should leave a job and how long it will take you to find another.

How to prepare a résumé.

What you should do about boredom.

Why you may not be promoted even though you have done a fine job.

What is the difference between working hard and being a workaholic.

And dozens of other things you should know about the world of work.

Actually there are listed in this book 258 techniques, tactics and strategies for protecting your job.

To begin . . .

The purpose of this book is to teach you how to protect your most valuable asset—your job.

In good times or bad, the same principles apply. In good times or bad, the same insights are important. Changing your job may be in your best interests. Losing your job is seldom in your best interests. Protecting a good job is always in your best interests.

This book contains the kind of information and experience I would have liked to have had when I began my career thirty years ago. It is also the result of interviews conducted by Joanne Summerfield with many people: personnel directors, executive recruiters, organization-wise middle managers, lawyers, labor specialists and chief executives. But mostly the book is based on my own thirty years as an organization man. The stories are largely mine, dredged from those years. They are all true, though names have been changed, identities disguised, to protect both the innocent and the guilty. Some of these stories are humorous, but their purpose is serious.

Most organizations try to treat people fairly. Most organizations are aware of the importance of the job to the individual.

After all, in private enterprise organizations, we are all job-holders, even high officers and chief executives, whose jobs may be more at hazard than anyone else's.

I was fortunate to work for two world-famous organizations over the period of my career as an organization man—with one for ten years, with the other for twenty years—and my experience with them was nothing but good, despite my own substantial shortcomings and annoying tendency toward independence and extracurricular creative activity. They managed to find something useful in my esoteric talents and put up with me in good times and bad for a substantial part of my life.

Besides my partner, Joanne Summerfield, president of Today's World, Inc., to whose interviewing, testing and validating talents I have been beholden for many years, I would like to express my appreciation to the following, who gave us both advice and commentary on the world we have explored: David W. Ewing, Managing Editor, *Harvard Business Review,* Henry Gunders, Co-Chairman, Price Waterhouse, Robert M. Maynard, National Director, Human Resources, Price Waterhouse, Ulric R. Sullivan, Attorney, Price Waterhouse, Jack Kielty, Earley Kielty and Associates, Executive Recruiters, Dr. Lyman K. Steil, President Communication Development, Inc., Alfred G. Feliu, Attorney specializing in Employment Relations, Alfred T. Jackson, Director, Employment Counseling, National Broadcasting Company, Julia Kearney, Editor, *Manager,* Southwestern Bell, Valkyr Branker, Administrator, Recruitment, NBC Personnel and Labor Relations, Roberta Oster, National Broadcasting Company, and Albert R. Smith, Jr., Vice President, Corporate Banking, Connecticut National Bank.

We also showed the manuscript to the chairmen or chief executive officers of four large corporations throughout the country and have taken into account their comments.

This book is dedicated to you who work for a living and to the enhancement and enjoyment of your greatest asset, your job.

GEORGE DE MARE

□

YOUR JOB
—Your Single
Most Valuable Asset

Most of us spend thirty or more years on the job. We spend most of our waking hours on the job. The job is our single most valuable asset. The job usually generates our livelihood. We build our marriage, our household, the rearing of our children and their education on it. We often build our status, our place in the world on it. We build many of our friendships and companionships on it. We get many of the most valuable experiences and much of the knowledge of life and the world through it.

Yet how many of us handle our job well? How many of us show the skill and respect our job deserves? How many of us treat our job with the intelligence and care it deserves? How many of us assess our job rationally in the context of our lives—then, if we find ourselves wanting, seek to improve ourselves, and if the job is found wanting, seek to improve it or to find another?

These are questions we must ask ourselves at all stages of our working lives. In our world and our economy, with a highly developed culture, jobs have become extremely complex, not only in terms of skills and experience but also in working and environmental relationships. Jobs have moved away from simple, structural skills based on apprenticeship to complex, unstructured white-collar work positions that demand education, the ability to handle professional and managerial work of a very high order and the ability to understand people and be able to communicate and get along with them.

Jobs turn into careers and careers into lives, and most of the jobs this book deals with are those that become careers.

Jobs that Turn into Careers

The people we interviewed and whose stories and precepts we have collected for you are people who deal mostly with jobs that turn into careers. Several are chief executives of corporations, large and small; several are directors of personnel with a special responsibility for the human resources of their organizations, for the jobs and careers of their companies; several are successful managers, who shared their own experiences in years of work holding varied jobs and have made a career of their work. Several are executive recruiters, who specialize in finding the right people for executive positions, and we also talked with labor leaders and two union executives.

Over the years, as the job progresses, as skills and knowledge increase, as understanding of the total impact of the work is gained, as one moves to new jobs demanding greater skill and knowledge, a career is developed.

The career may demand the skills and experience of more than one job, though you may remain with the same organization. Those in professions, of course, have jobs, but they are essentially careers demanding from the first all the education, planning, studying and experience of careers. A career demands more than the job itself. It demands planning, studying and the consideration of what jobs one should take to gain the experience and development needed for a career.

A career may demand that you take a job that pays less than the one you are able to command or now have in order to gain some experience or knowledge or skill you will need later on. Every soldier who makes a career in the armed forces would like to have seen action. A marketing director might like to have tried being a salesman. An executive will boast of his days on the shop floor or in the field. Careers are based on jobs and on the right jobs well done, on the experience they give and on the discipline, the dedication, the sacrifices that jobs demand.

What we learned we have dealt with under the four major elements of handling a job well—the work, the relationships, the outside environment and the possibilities of help where necessary and appropriate. Under each area, we have selected what to us are the most revealing and useful anecdotes and advice on that subject. Sociologists and social scientists have spent years and produced treatises and books on work motivation, human relationships and our economic environment, and much of their work has been important and revelatory. But there are more than 100 million of us in the work force of our economy, and the getting and holding of a job always comes down to the problems and challenges of these four areas: the work, the relationships, the outside environment, and where and how to get help.

The first area of doing a good job: The work

The first area—the work itself—seems simple and straightforward. You take a job. If you are a beginner, it is a simple job. You are on a line or you are an office boy or you add up figures or you count the items of merchandise or you wait on the customer or you get coffee for the advertising manager and sit in on copy sessions and get the props for production or you keep the engineering records for the foreman or you throw the morning paper on the doorstep.

But what you are learning is the work itself, the way to do it, the way it should be done, the way it is done in that particular organization, in that particular community at that particular period. What is difficult in the beginning of any job is the simplicity of the work, the ease with which it is mastered and the boredom of repetition. How do you justify to yourself the small part of your talents and knowledge and skill used by any entry-level job? How do you escape the terrible boredom? We asked our veterans and experts these questions. The answers reflected two approaches: (1) Look at the job in the context of the whole enterprise and (2) prepare yourself for the work above this job level.

The problem, these experts told us, was one of attitude. The work counts, of course, or the organization would not pay good money for it, but the willingness and cheerfulness of the jobholder count too. However, one can be a sucker here, so we discuss these matters in more detail in our next area: relationships. But in the area of the work itself, our experts and veterans stated over and over again that it will help if you know the value of the job itself in the context of the whole enterprise and if you take steps to incorporate more of the enterprise's needs into your job. In the beginning this is difficult. As you move up, it becomes more feasible and more essential.

A third precept from our experts and veterans on the area of the work itself is: *Never let your job narrow you.*

If the job is too trivial and boring for you and, for the time being, you cannot do better, go outside to other studies and activities. A bad job, a trivial job, a job that wastes the jobholder's abilities must be supplemented outside the working hours and the workplace until a better one can be found.

We all instinctively realize this, but our experts tell us it is surprising how many people allow themselves to be trapped in a life-wasting job. The job is one area of our lives where we may have more control over our progress than we believe. This book is dedicated to giving you the advice and knowledge of experts to help you gain that control.

The second area of doing a good job: The relationships

More people have failed at or lost potentially good jobs through not being able to fit in or establish good relationships on the job than for any other reason. One executive recruiter told us that in a study his firm made, only 15 percent of those who lost their jobs were fired for incompetence and that by far the highest percentage lost their jobs because of poor relationships, or, as they sometimes liked to put it, office politics.

The truth is, as most of us instinctively know, relationships are the essence of any job. Most of us can do the work, but how many of us give the care, attention and the respect to the relationships, the people, the community, the ambience in which we work that they deserve? In an organization, no job is done alone. We are all dependent on what others do and on how others think. We are all dependent on what respect we are able to earn in that community, for an organization is a community, and we live and die by what our community thinks of us at work just as we do at home or anywhere else. We may think, as often happens in entry-level jobs, that we are here only to do the work and get our pay and get home. If we do the work well or even adequately, that is all that should count. We are not here to be loved or applauded. Unfortunately, it is not that simple. We are there also as part of an organization, with all that implies.

For many this is a hard truth to swallow. We all want to be independent, to be free. We want to do a job and earn our pay and go home at night to the wife or husband and kids and forget the rest. A job is not supposed to be a Faustian bargain. You're not supposed to sell your soul to the Company Store. You may have indentured yourself, but only for the work and nothing else.

The truth is you are in an enterprise with other people within the ambience of an organization that has built up customs, traditions, beliefs and ways of looking at things, and if you have no respect or understanding of the people, the customs, the traditions or beliefs, no matter how good you are in your work, you will not last long.

You may call this "office politics" if you wish, but our experts and veterans were unanimous on the crucial importance of attitude and on being able to respect and enjoy the world in which you do your job even with all its stupidities and defects. Jobs are jobs, but organizations are not just organizations—they are communities of people, and you must learn to become a part of them. Necessity has often forced us into jobs in organizations that we find hard to relate to, but relate to them we must, not only to the boss and the officers but to others also, if we are to do a job. In every community, in every organization, there are people of superior talent, ability, personality and sensitivity who have become what sociologists call opinion leaders. They may or may not be found in high positions, but to do a good job in any complex undertaking, you will need to get their respect and support. So you must study your organization, learn who the opinion leaders are and establish good relationships with those with whom you work. As one personnel director summed up the relationship problem: "You must become one of us."

This is not always easy. Even in organizations where we find ourselves in an environment we like and with people we respect, there will be problems in the area of relationships, and since this is the most complex and difficult aspect of holding a job, we have given this area perhaps the greatest concentration in this book.

The third area of doing a good job: Knowing about the outside work world

This third area increases your ability to do a good job by giving you perspective on your job in the marketplace, how it is rated, how it is valued and what is being done by others in terms of improvement or changes in the functions or work you perform. Second, it gives you perspective on your own value in the marketplace. You need to know your economic and social value in order to assess yourself within your own organization. Sometimes you will find your expectations and evaluations too high, sometimes too low, but knowing them in the larger economy will help you do a better job and be realistic in your work progress. Third, getting outside into the market-place and making the acquaintance of others in the work world will help you build up a network of those who have jobs and positions similar to yours, those who work in widely diverse organizations, a network that can enrich your knowledge and experience through the exchange of information and ideas, through assistance to others and through the building of outside friendships in the work world that can stand you in good stead later on.

The fourth area: Possible remedies and help if you have been unfairly treated

The job—the work one does for pay—is so important in the life of the community that our culture has not only supported it with custom and tradition but also with regulations designed to protect people from unfair treatment. In our society the union concept has been supported, and we have also tried to prevent people from being unfairly treated in the work world because of race, sex or age. We have gathered and summarized a few representative cases that reveal the costs and benefits of using these remedies where they are appropriate.

Careers that Turn into Lives

The job that becomes a career was not long ago a lifetime occupation. The career—that is the job or series of jobs that turn into an occupation—is still in most cases a lifetime matter. However, as mobility has increased and as people live longer and reach the retirement age on their jobs at what seems the height of their vigor and experience, an increasing number of us have more than one career.

Women who raise families and at the same time or after the children have grown take a job may be said to have two careers, the more arduous and important one perhaps being that of raising a family. But men, particularly those with unusual ability and experience, also are increasingly moving from one career to a related one to fulfill their talents and round out an active life.

Nothing is sadder than the retirement of an active, vigorous personality from a position of authority and fruitful work to an idleness that leaves those talents and that energy unused. We are all familiar with the ravages of loss of a job and a career in terms of broken spirits and wasted life. We have seen the once young, once vigorous sixty- or seventy-year-old turn into a tired old man, ready to die or hanging on only to complain about the world and to dream of days when he was younger and respected for what he was doing.

Now we are all becoming aware of the importance of our having a job or a significant activity that will last us a lifetime, and most of us are beginning to learn how to prepare for so-called retirement. What those who are successful at this learn is to prepare for another job, another career that can use what we have learned and built up in skills and experience.

Often now people also move in midlife to a second job and career that uses more or different aspects of their abilities and experience: the executive or the professional becomes a teacher in a university; the professor moves into politics or starts a consultation practice of his own. All these moves are usually life-enhancing to the person and good for our society and economy, which more and more require varied and highly talented work to keep our life-styles and standard of living at their present levels.

This book, then, is dedicated to those who love a job, who love their work and learn to do it over a lifetime. The advice and stories we have garnered from our experts and veterans should provide some insights for those who are taking their first job, for those who hold jobs now and for those who are approaching that time when they should be preparing for a second job that will last them a lifetime.

Your Job

Work and love—the two most important preoccupations of human life—we dedicate this book to the job, that unit of our work for which our society is willing to pay. We hope the advice given will enhance your enjoyment and your profit in the greatest single economic asset you will ever own—your job.

PART I

□

ARE YOU TAKING YOUR JOB FOR GRANTED?

The first time you may come to grips with the value and importance of the job in you life may be the most difficult and crucial time of all—the time when your job is in danger. There are many reasons your job can be on the line, a great many of them preventable or salvageable, others perhaps beyond your ability or the organization's means to remedy. You should be able to spot and understand these situations, however, and you should know what can be done.

The stories told here of danger situations are representative of what can and does happen. Only the names are changed and identities concealed.

The Sudden Silence

The speaker, Keith Moran, is the forty-year-old executive of a large manufacturing organization in the warehouse operations section. He is a heavyset, brooding, cigar-smoking man—and something of a bear. He is a self-made man. He had been with the company almost ten years and had worked his way up from the loading platform. He was very proud of that and would push it in the face of new men coming into the executive group, who, as he put it, had never got their hands dirty or loaded for six hours straight in an emergency to get the trucks rolling to a disaster area.

3

He almost met his Waterloo when a new director was placed in charge of the division that included his department and his old boss, whom he admired, was transferred out. He resented the new boss and, in a crucial display of his usual outspokenness, he had a memorable scene. He describes what happened.

*   *   *

This guy didn't know beans about warehouse management. It's typical of the company. They want to give some fancy-pants guy they're grooming a taste of reality and they off-load him on us. Well, I made a mistake an' I admit it.

The guy tried to be friendly and I wasn't having any, an' I told him to his face he didn't know beans about this kind of operation and that's how it started. He was one of those quiet guys you can't trust. He didn't react much, but I noticed things changed. First of all, I wasn't invited to the monthly meetings no more. Then I noticed that some of the foremen weren't turnin' in the reports or givin' me the word the way they used to, and when you talk to guys like Callahan and Sparks they wasn't kidding around the way they used to.

All this begun happening over a period of time, before I really noticed it. I don't usually notice crap like that. But it was like a sudden silence, where you find you don't know what's goin' on and nobody is sayin' anything to you that means anything. You kind of get cut off—not just from the official stuff, though that's bad enough, but also from the grapevine, the rumor mill where all the real poop comes from.

Now I been here ten years and I'm a good warehouseman if I do say so myself. I did long haul once— before that, had my own truck. I know warehouse, know how to get good service, how to keep 'em from stealing you blind, know how to handle inventory and all that, an' I hate bullshit, an' all you get upstairs is

4

bullshit, especially with this new guy. He wasn't like old Don Mack, who spoke right out and told you off when he didn't like somethin'. But now all I get is this sudden silence.

So I sit myself down an' say to myself: "Keith, you may be in trouble, big trouble. Nobody talkin' to you, guys avoidin' you, an' all because of this fancy pants. An' it ain't no laughing matter. You're forty years old with a wife an' four kids an' you don't want to go back on the trucks again—you're gettin' too old for long haul an' maybe this ain't such a bad job. An' I earned it. What am I goin' to do?"

*   *   *

What Keith Moran should have done was get an appointment and go in and talk to the new boss, ask him what he had done wrong, how he could improve his operation. This he did not do and because of his nature could not bring himself to do. It was a very near thing. He was not fired but he was in effect demoted and lost much of his influence. His bad temper, his rough ways, his outspokenness and tactlessness had brought him to the edge. His loyalty and competence finally won out, since the new executive was a fair-minded man. But Keith Moran suffered one of the sure signs that his job was on the line—the sudden silence. Our experts agree that keeping open communications is a necessity in protecting and enhancing a job.

"Let's Have a Heart-to-Heart"

Randy Jordan is a twenty-six-year-old insurance salesman. He is a good-looking young man, articulate and well-dressed, and with two years of college. He makes a nice appearance. He had been on the job one year when this episode occurred.

*   *   *

I fell for this line about making so much a year and being your own man. Also they train you. The man-

5

ager I'm assigned to, Burt Taylor, is one of these executive types and full of bullshit most of the time. He's an old-line salesman.

"You've been to college a couple of years. You know a lot of classmates who are good insurance prospects," he says. "Then there's your family and relatives who can suggest people to you. You'll have no trouble making up good lists and they'll give you names in your territory to call on. And so you build up a bunch of clients that'll give you a nice fat cushion for the rest of your life."

I did fine in the beginning. I got my list together and I gave it the old college try, and I sold better than my quota. But all their bullshit began to get to me, all this stuff about protecting your loved ones and this and that. And selling yourself as the guide and counselor and we'll tailor your policy to your means and your needs. It was bullshit. We start trying to sell them twenty-year life, then whole life, then all the way through, and if nothing works we sell term and we have fancy names and tables you wouldn't believe, except you do, and I just got tired of the bullshit.

So I kind of took it easy for a while. And then there was my attitude in the office. So I get this call on a Monday morning. It's from good old Burt Taylor: "Come in tomorrow at nine-thirty. We need to have a heart-to-heart."

For God's sake—a heart-to-heart. So there I was in my go-to-meeting clothes and my shoes polished—the way I hit my classmates and family friends with the old spiel and mortality tables. But Old Burt Taylor, his usual soft-voiced, smooth self, kind of surprised me, and I've been thinking about what he said. I'm giving it a lot of thought.

"If you didn't have it, Randy," he said, "we'd have had this heart-to-heart six months ago. We can tell

6

when a guy can't make it and we don't waste his time or ours. Well, you can make it, but I'm not sure you want to. And so I'm laying it on the line to you. This is a tough business, Randy. It has its rewards and they're big ones but it's not for the fainthearted or the smart asses or for the know-it-alls. It's for those who can help people take care of their future. And you've got to believe in it. If I didn't believe in it, I wouldn't be here, Randy. I'm no dummy. I didn't invest nearly eight years of my life in something that gives me a bellyache every time I come in in the morning. Nor did I give sometimes ten, twelve hours a day to something I looked down on.

Now you showed promise. You have the touch. You could maybe get rich in this business. But these last few months you've just been going through the motions. The results show. Now I don't know what's wrong and I can't help you. It's hard to sell somebody something you don't believe in. I'd like to keep you but I'm not going to try. If you're good and we like you, we're going to give you the breaks and you're going up. If you're good and we don't like you, we're going to keep you and maybe give you the breaks. If you're good potential and we like you and you don't come through, we're not going to keep you. And there it is. So now you've got fair warning. You've got three months to think about it and to come through on your quota."

*   *   *

Randy Jordan came through in the three months allotted him and he put on a good show of his change of heart. But he is still not sure he wants to stay. He is not married and he can probably find another, equally good job. But the heart-to-heart shook him up. He had not thought he could ever be fired. He came of a generation who had been told they were golden and that any organization was lucky to get them. It had not turned out that way. He finds himself somewhat disillusioned about the world but he realizes he is going to have to find out what he really wants to do, how he really wants to live. Meanwhile he is working hard. He no longer likes Burt Taylor, but he respects him despite himself. He knows Burt Taylor means business. He knows he is going to have to produce for Burt Taylor if he wants to stay. And he knows this job has got to have his respect if he is going to make it.

"Is Something Wrong?"

Eileen Wheeler is an executive secretary to the vice-president of marketing of a large consumer products company. She has become wedded to the company and feels a sort of proprietary interest in everything that happens there. She is in her early forties; an early marraige ended in divorce and she has been with the company for eighteen years. She has been with Mr. Trevor, the marketing vice-president for two years. She took Mrs. Bellamy's place. Mrs. Bellamy was a highly respected, very influential executive secretary—middle-aged when she started, like Eileen, and quiet, impersonal and friendly. Eileen has become possessive, irritable and difficult. On a Wesnesday afternoon, she receives a call from Genevieve Morton, a young personnel manager whom Eileen considers something of an upstart. Genevieve has only been with the company five years. Would Eileen please come down to the personnel department, Genevieve asks. An important matter has come up. Eileen replies she is very busy. Mr. Trevor has her on some important work. She can't come now. What is it Genevieve wants. Genevieve is silent a moment. Then she says, "Mr. Trevor has asked me to speak to you."

*   *   *

I've given the best years of my life to this company and this is what happens. I don't know whether I can go on. But they're not going to get rid of me that easy. It's not like the old days when I worked for Mr. Hanrahan. He was a gentleman, no nosing around after these new girls they're hiring now—no nonsense. So I go down to see this Genevieve Morton, a snippy young woman they've got in personnel, and she asks me to sit down a minute in this fancy office she's got, but I tell her I'm too busy to sit down, to tell me what she wants, so I can get back to work. But she says "Please, Eileen." So I sit down. And she opens up saying, "Eileen, is anything wrong?" And I say, "Yes, there's plenty wrong, but why are you asking?"

"Well," she says,"Mr. Trevor would like to have you transferred to some other post." So I just looked at her. I was in shock, "Transferred?" I said. "Yes," she answered. "He feels you don't like the pressures they're under in his department, and he needs someone who has a little more patience and, well, who will be easier on those trying to get in to see him. Apparently some of the poeple working for him feel that you shut them out and that you're a little brusque with them." Then she says to me again, "Eileen, is something wrong?"

"I'll tell you what's wrong, Miss Morton," I said. I was furious. "Mr. Trevor seems to be carrying on with one of the new girls down there, and I think it's disgraceful. He's a married man. This would not have been tolerated in the days when I worked for Mr. Hanrahan."

This little snit just sits there looking at me.

"Eileen," she says at last. She sounds tired. "I don't think Mr. Trevor's personal life is either your or my business. However, I guess it's best for all concerned if we transfer you to someone else."

"I think Mr. Trevor's behavior should be brought to the attention of the proper authorities," I said.

9

"Eileen," the girl said, "you've been with this company eighteen years. One of the few ways you can terminate that long relationship is to make wild accusations like the one you've just made about an officer of the company. I doubt that you could substantiate your statement, and in any case it seems irrelevant to Mr. Trevor's job. I want you to think over carefully what you're saying and, if the moral climate of the organization does not agree with you, consider resigning. In any case, Eileen, you will be transferred to my department until we can find a suitable post for you. You will have the week off to think over the problems that seem to have arisen. Then you are to come in and see me and we'll work out a transfer or a settlement. Mr. Trevor is very concerned about you but he is carrying a heavy load and he needs someone more supportive."

Can you imagine? Can you just imagine! I don't know what I'm going to do, but they're not going to get rid of me this easily.

* * *

Eileen Wheeler was persuaded to accept a transfer. She was also counseled by the company doctor, who persuaded her to see someone about her increased disillusionment with the organization and the world and her bouts of depression and anger.

"I Sometimes Think You're Not Happy Around Here"

Vern Max is a programmer in a fast-growing high-tech organization. He is a cynical, balding man with a lopsided smile and a sharp tongue but is considered a crackerjack in his field. This is what happened to him.

* * *

They want you to salute the flag in this outfit and that's not for me. Every Friday evening we have a

10

beer bust, and the boys gather at the old corral, as they call the lab, and Jack treats us all to beer and barbecue, all two hundred of us and those that have wives or girl friends bring them too. I suppose it's all very democratic and good fellowship and all, but Jesus Christ, what if you don't want to see the same old faces every week? What if you want to forget the goddamn hassle once in a while? What if you'd rather take off and go to Las Vegas for a weekend or just work out chess moves or just be by yourself?

I'm a loner. When I work, I work, but I don't want to read a policy manual, a ten commandments or any of the rest of the crap Jack has set up for this outfit. So on a Tuesday afternoon—I suppose he was working up to it all weekend and Monday—he comes to my work place—we don't have offices here—and asks if he can talk to me. I say, "Jack, you can always talk to me. What's on your mind?"

He comes in and sits down. Jack's a tall, intense guy, good smile and all, very good systems man, first rate, but underneath all that good-guy stuff you can see he's a Moral Majority type to his toes. He tries to play the easygoing yet gung-ho boss. He tries to be one of the boys but he's the boss and he has a whim of iron underneath it all. He always asks your advice, but you know damn well that's just a gesture. I don't know. Maybe I'm getting cynical in my old age. Hell, I guess I've always been cynical.

So Jack says, "Vern, I sometimes think you're not happy around here."

I wait.

"I get the feeling," he says, "that you can't relate to what's going down here. You're a great programmer and everybody respects you, but they feel you don't like them and you make them feel put down."

"In other words, Jack," I say, "you want me to

11

move on. We can cut the crap," I say. "We're grown men. I'll take a walk across the street. They can use me there—if you don't louse it up."

"You'll get nothing but the highest recommendation from me, Vern," he says. These are nice guys even if they're full of crap.

"Will you shake hands?" Jack asks.

"Sure," I said, "but I won't be at the beer bust Friday and I won't be coming back Monday, so let's get everything settled by then."

"Agreed," Jack said.

* * *

Vern Max went to work for a huge, rather impersonal conglomerate in their data processing center. He puts in his time and keeps to himself.

"Joe, That Was a Great Job You Did, but . . ."

If a project fails or a program goes out of fashion, those at the head of it suffer. Joe Cantine tells what happened to him.

* * *

All it was was politics. The project could have paid off if they'd given it a chance, but no, they got cold feet when the overruns began to show up, so they jettisoned everything. Almost three-quarters of a million down the drain. Sure, there were a few defects and sure we were projecting a fairly heavy overrun, but in a project like this, with a potentially heavy payoff, you've got to expect these things. You've got to take risks.

This company is all short run, quick payoff, no staying power. But I think it was Hilburn did it. When he came in, it was as a hatchet man—cost cutting—and he didn't care how he cut. Sure, we were a bit over-expanded and this project was going to be a year overdue, and sure I got pretty hot under the collar when he started pushing us, but we could have brought it in and we could have gotten it to market. No, it was all politics.

You get caught in a political situation like this and you're done for. It's all politics around here anyhow. While Fred was in charge, I knew I had a friend and I was in solid. When Hilburn came in, he wanted his own people in and his own projects. That's how I see it. I suppose we could have done better with the project. But the expectations were too high. The truth is it was oversold. And not by me. I was just the guy put in charge. And now I'm the fall guy. I'm tarred with that failure.

And this is the worst time for this kind of thing to happen. They're having a cut of "positions," and it's beginning to look to me as if my former position is one that's being cut. This is a tough time. They've already cut ten positions, which means at least ten of us are going to be out or transferred. I should never have taken that project. I should have stayed with my old position, where I could defend my turf. I didn't play my cards right. Now I've got nobody to go to, nowhere to go. They're all under orders to cut. I can feel it already. Pretty soon, Hilburn's going to call me in and say, "Joe, that was a great job you did, but it just didn't pan out, and I'm afraid we don't have a position for you anymore." I don't know. I guess I'll just have to wait and see. It's all politics.

* * *

Joe Cantine was right. He was one of those who were eventually let go. This was a very tough time for middle managers. What should he have done? Our advisers suggest he should have looked around in the company immediately to see where they might really be able to use him. He should have analyzed the experience he had gained on the special project to see where it might be relevant in some other group. At the same time he should have begun picking up his outside contacts to see what the job market was in his field and have begun to let others outside know that he is looking around. It is always easier to get another job, if you still have a job, our advisers say. In any event, Joe Cantine should not have just waited around and hoped for the best, saying, "It's all just politics."

"Our Department Is Being Reorganized"

There are situations where the reason for letting someone go is not clear and a more or less specious reason is given by the executive. Calvin Baker is still not sure why he was let go. He worked for three years in the public relations department of a large food company and generally was more talented and productive than most of those in that department. They are keeping on a lot of less talented, less productive people.

* * *

I suppose I must have made Fatso Flanagan nervous or something, though he seemed to like me. It's certainly not because they're trying to reorganize or get rid of deadwood. They seem to be keeping all the deadwood. Not that I'm any live wire myself. We're a very ordinary, run-of-the-mill group. I'd understand it better if they had fired all of us. So I keep asking myself: Why me?

It can't be the work. I can do stories and captions for the company papers and publications as well as the next. Could it have been the takeoff I did on the company picnic? Or the edited version of the president's year-end message, where I showed what the president was really saying. I only let Manny and a few others see them. And as for bloopers, it wasn't I who made the obscene typo in the caption under the photo show-

14

ing Isabelle Howell of personnel playing tennis. The caption should have read, "A good play," but someone left out the *p* and that issue became a classic. It wasn't I who did the sloppy job of proofreading on a four-color Christmas-issue cover of our quarterly, showing the Child in the manger and the three Wise Men. The caption read, "Babe in the Manager." I mean this can happen to anybody, and I didn't notice our editor Fatso Flanagan hanging himself. Nor are they letting him go. I guess they like to have him around to torture. He always looks as if the world were coming to an end. He always looks as if he took the stuff we do more seriously than the rest of us do. Maybe I don't have that sincere look you need around here. Anyway, this is what happened.

Fatso calls me in. Fatso's not a bad guy. He's a big, heavy, roly-poly with this serious, worried look. He always looks as if he's sitting on a powder keg and someone has just lit a match. He's an old newspaper man and proud of it. He comes on as if he were a free spirit, likes to talk about the good old days when he was on a big city newspaper. But he's strictly a company man. He'd sell his mother for the company, and he's scared shitless that something might go wrong, so of course it always does. Yet they love him up the line. The head of the department, a real sadist, James Gestro—Mr. Gestro to us—has been with the company thirty years. He came up from dog food. He likes to see Fatso sweat, and Fatso does plenty of sweating.

Now don't get me wrong. I hate to lose this job. It's easy for a guy like me who's going to write the Great American Novel. It's fun once in a while, and I like the others all right, even though some of them are worse goof-offs than me.

So Fatso sits me down and he leans forward in his creaky swivel chair that's going to give way one of

15

these days and puts his two hundred and fifty pounds on the floor, and says:

"Calvin, I've bad news. They've cut us down. They've cut us down, Calvin boy. Our department is being reorganized, and the Great White Father has decreed I let you and two others go. I hate to do it, Calvin boy. Truly I do. You're one of the best writers we have, but . . .''

Well, there it was. I suppose there were a lot of reasons to let me go, but I'll never know what the real one was or why me rather than some of the other goof-offs in our group. Anyhow, back to the drawing board . . .

* * *

Calvin may have been let go because his larky approach to his work upset the timid editor or because his irreverence came to the attention of Mr. Gestro. Or for some minor sin he himself is not aware of. He will never know. And while it was painful for him to lose this job, he will be better off, given his temperament, in a more open, less structured environment. Meanwhile, our advisers say he should request enough time with the company to find himself another job.

You Know, a Person with your Qualifications is in Great Demand Now . . ."

A middle-management executive in the financial services area, Hal Harper, is speaking.

* * *

It was a Friday afternoon when it happened. I don't know why it came as such a shock. We should have been prepared for it. We had just been acquired by one of the larger conglomerates and, while we had all been assured that things would be better than ever now that we were going to be part of Octopus, Incor-

16

porated, I'd been around long enough to know there would have to be changes and some of us were going to be hurt.

The truth is you tend to hide your head in the sand. You tend to swallow all the garbage they give you in these acquisition situations about the increased opportunities, the greater need for competent managers, for people who know how to plan and organize and so on. You want to believe and so you go along. The irony is that three years ago, when I received an offer from another organization, they didn't want to let me go. They met the other company's offer and gave me a promotion. They talked about loyalty and the great future I had in the organization. I was golden.

Now it's all a different story. Now we've been absorbed by Big Daddy, and Big Daddy is consolidating, and guess who in which organization is getting the preferred treatment. Our company was much smaller and there was inevitable duplication and it's our people who are generally getting the shaft. So on this Friday afternoon—the worst time you can do this to a person—I was called in by Herb Newman, the acquiring company's department head in my area. Herb is the new big boy in our area. He's always friendly and affable. He's a tall wiry guy with glinting rimless glasses, always smiling, always complimentary. But some of us now refer to him as the Grim Reaper. I guess I suspected what was coming.

"You know, Hal," Newman says, "a man with your qualifications is in great demand now. You're the kind of top-flight man who will have no trouble placing himself. Also, I'm going to hate to lose you, but there's no help for it. Ed Gross is being put in charge of your group, and I simply have no place else to put a man of your abilities and qualifications. Believe me, I've tried, but the orders are out from upstairs and

17

that's that. Now we'll make you a generous settlement, and we'll give you plenty of time to make your
change . . .''

I didn't hear the rest of it. The shock was too great. I
just sat there, looking at this smiling idiot. I saw his
mouth moving but I couldn't hear anything. I don't
really remember anything until I found myself standing outside Herb's office. I can tell you that weekend
was the worst in my life.

I'm angry with myself. I should have been looking
around when we first heard we were going to be acquired. I shouldn't have believed all this opportunity
and loyalty baloney. But I spent ten years of my life in
this organization. I kept my nose clean. I did a good
job for them, and you can take your loyalty now and
shove it up your ass. What they're doing for me after
ten years besides giving me the old heave-ho is they've
got me and four others of us with an outplacement
firm. Believe me, I'm going to keep my eyes open and
my loyalty to myself after this!

*   *   *

*Hal Harper's reaction is a common one. "How could he
have protected his job?" we asked our experts. Most agreed
that there was no sure way, where staff has to be reduced
because of acquisitions and mergers or recessions, but they
did agree that if he had followed the principles outlined in
Part III, "Relationships—Thirty Things You Should Know
about an Organization and Its People," and had kept his
contacts outside the organization as outlined in Part IV,
"The Outside Work World," he would have been in a position to consolidate his relationships in the new organization
or to move quickly to another job before the ax fell. In either
case, he would be prepared and able to make an adjustment
in his own best interests.*

What are the answers, then, to these seven "symptoms"

that you may be in trouble in your job. The answers are not as simple as the situation indicated. There may be any of a dozen or so variables in each case. You may be required to change habits and ways of looking at your job and your career that were built up over the years and are now placing you in a less competitive position in the world you aspire to.

Let these symptoms then serve as a springboard to the parts which follow with their situations and instructional material: twenty things you should know about doing a job, thirty things you should know about an organization and its people, twenty-nine things you should know about whether you have the right job and are being paid enough and things you can do if you are unfairly treated.

PART II

□

THE WORK
—Twenty Things You Should Know About Doing a Job

Work means much more in a person's life than making a living. Besides occupying most of our waking hours, it enables us, according to sociologists and psychologists, to build and define ourselves as individuals and is one of the two major preoccupations—love being the other—which alone are absolutely essential to a fulfilled life.

"Work," one of those interviewed by Studs Terkel in his seminal book, *Working,* says "is an essential part of being alive. Your work is your identity. It tells you who you are."

Work has been defined as goal-oriented activity that has a social or economic value, and it involves skill as well as experience. A job is a piece of work for which we are paid, and the function itself has values for the worker. You tend to assess yourself as a person, as others tend to assess you, often largely on how good you are in your job.

This area of your job, the work, is thus of major importance to you. Whether you feed steel to the scarfing machine, type letters or manage a large division, the development of the skills required, whether physical, mental or social, forms the base of your job and in the fullness of your career can be both absorbing and sometimes overwhelming. In the entry-level job, the problem is usually how little of your potential is used, while in the higher reaches of your work, the problem may be the stretching of the limits of your skills. Nevertheless, at all

23

stages of your working life, the work itself and your skills and abilities, as shown in these twenty examples of things you should know about doing a job, are of prime importance to you.

This section offers the combined wisdom of our advisers on twenty core subjects having to do with your work itself. These nuggets of advice are offered on subjects most often puzzling, overlooked or not sufficiently understood by those of us who hold jobs. They deal with common situations and how to face them.

Are You Competent?

Jim Ellsworth was called in by Cal Knowlton, the department head, for the annual staff review.

"How do you think you're doing, Jim?" Cal asked, looking at the dossier before him. "Are you getting the drafting assignments on time?"

"I'm doing fine, Cal," Jim said. "Yes, of course. I have more work piled up than I can get to."

"Are they giving you more assignments than the others or are they more difficult?" Knowlton asked.

"Well, I don't think so," Jim answered. "I really don't know."

"Jim," Cal said, "your productivity in the group is a bit below average. I wonder whether you might talk to Art Landon and discuss how you might go about handling these assignments more expeditiously?"

"My productivity?" Jim said. "What do you mean?"

"The number of assignments completed per month is significantly below average," Cal said.

"I didn't know we had a quota to do!" Jim said. "We never did in the old days. We took 'em as they came and took our time and did 'em right."

24

"No more, Jim," Cal replied. "There are measurements of productivity in every department now. The measurement in your group is assignments completed with a weight given to the complexity of the job. If you look at the average in your group, you'll see that while your jobs have been weighed properly and the quality of your work is satisfactory, your productivity is below average. I'm sure you can remedy that. Talk to Landon sometime this week, will you?"

Jim Ellsworth was flabbergasted. He was an old-timer and had not realized that, in terms of his job, he was becoming incompetent. He had not informed himself of the measurements of competence in his work.

One of the key questions you must ask yourself in terms of the work you are doing is, "Am I competent?"

To answer that question you must know three things:

1. How does the organization measure competence in my area?

2. How do those to whom I report judge competence in my job? What characteristics of my work do they feel are important and how do they assess them?

3. What impact does my job or my work have on the total enterprise?

It is, of course, easy to measure certain types of jobs or to see how they play a role in the organization's profitability. A salesman can usually be measured by the number and size of the orders he secures and a worker on the assembly line can be measured by an agreed-upon productivity quota, but as jobs become more complex and professional, as you move higher in the organization, your own measure of your competence becomes more difficult to perceive, and the organization's measure of your competence more complex. How do you measure the work of a research scientist or the work of higher management? Yet their competence is assessed, whether the measurements are subjective or not. The head of a division must plan and estimate the results of that division's contribution to the organization and meet the goal agreed upon with the head of the organization. The chief executive of a company is measured by the company's profitability, return on assets and a number of other measures, as well as by how this compares with similar organizations in his industry. One of the characteristics he must have—one which often is not mentioned but cannot be over looked—is luck. Providence is unfortunately not an equal opportunity employer, and the higher you go, the more important it is that you be at the right place at the right time, that your skills be those required by the corporation for its prosperity, that your intuition be sound when there is no real way to know which way the wind will blow. At this level, the measure of competence is results.

A well-managed organization generally has job descriptions for each position, from that of the president and chief executive officer to those of the most basic operations. If your organization does not have a job description of your position, you have the opportunity to study your work and produce a good description of your job for your own purposes. A good job description gives you a better understanding of your work and its value to the organization. If your organization does have a job description of your work, study it and be aware of its demands and requirements. It will give you one clue as to how your job will be measured.

Example of a Job Description

MANAGER OF SYSTEMS AND PROGRAMMING

REPORTS TO DIRECTOR OF ELECTRONIC DATA PROCESSING.

Responsibilities

—Plans, organizes and controls the activities of systems analysts and programmers in the development and imple-

---

26

mentation of new or revised computer-oriented information processing systems and procedures.

—Maintains technical responsibility for the development of systems design specifications, program specification, program development and testing, and systems programming.

—Prepares progress reports for each development project that will display systems design and program development progress in terms of actual vs. estimated manpower and target date vs. percentage of completion.

—Establishes standards for system design documentation, program specification requirements, flow charting, programming procedures, including specification of program-language usage standards and program documentation.

—Collaborates with systems analysts and other technical personnel in performing equipment analysis, feasibility studies, applications system design and software package evaluation.

—Advises other departments on the technical problems associated with proposed systems and procedures.

—Reviews the design concepts of proposed systems to determine future manpower and equipment needs.

—Reviews and evaluates the work of the staff and prepares periodic performance reports for personnel evaluation.

—Reviews and evaluates new hardware and software products that may be of significance in the client's EDP environment. Makes appropriate recommendations when opportunities for utilization arise.

Background

The Manager of Systems and Programming should be an EDP professional who can successfully direct the productivity of a programming staff while keeping himself and his employees up-to-date. Requirements include at least four to seven years of heavy applications systems and programming experience as well as prior project leader/lead programmer responsibility. Multiple hardware and software experience is desirable as is some exposure to software maintenance. Third-generation-software utilization experience and project management experience are basic requirements. A college and/or advanced degree is desirable.

Some techniques, tactics and stratagems to consider

It would seem that finding out whether you are considered competent and are doing the job satisfactorily would be easy, but particularly in the case of those on the job for any length of time, this may not be the case. We tend to "know" when we are doing a good job by observing that the boss likes us and seems happy with what we are doing. The problem may arise when the boss moves on and a new boss comes in or when we suddenly find our group reorganized to take on expanded tasks or different operations. Our job may then be phased out because it is no longer adequate to the total enterprise.

Here are four tactics that will help you assess your competence on the job:

1. Ask your boss or others in the organization responsible for describing job functions or measuring them what are the elements in your job by which the work is measured.

2. Look at how well you meet these tests of competence. If you are below average or do not measure up to the tests, study ways in which these elements can be brought up to par.

3. Look at how your work affects other jobs and add this factor into your measure of job effectiveness.

4. If you can see ways of improving the effectiveness of your job, put them in a memo; then discuss them with those affected by them, including your boss, and if they are well received, implement them.

28

Skills

What are the skills required in your job?

Oddly enough, they may not necessarily be the skills you think you need or are most proud of or the skills others believe are essential to your work.

For example, an auditor in a large accounting firm, while he may need a good business and financial background, needs another major skill, not generally equated with his work. He needs unusual skill in communicating and getting along with people—a social skill. The reason: He deals with clients in a sensitive area, and unless those being audited trust him and will talk to him, he cannot do the job he was trained to do.

Three questions:

1. Are my skills still relevant to my job?
2. Are they up-to-date?
3. Are there additional skills I should acquire to move on?

Every job requires skill. Even shoveling coal, as Frederick Winslow Taylor, the father of work measurement and scientific management, showed. Skills may be physical, mental, professional, artistic or managerial. Society values and usually pays enormous sums for major skills. The great athlete, the pop singer, the Picasso of the art world, the major writer, the gifted chief executive of the most profitable company all command our admiration and the world's wealth. In our jobs, however, our less exalted skills are only part of the job, and the skills we began with may over time become irrelevant or even obsolete. In a rather chilling study made a few years ago by Samuel S. Dubin of Pennsylvania State University, the rate of obsolescence of several professions was assessed. In an interview the professor said: "Five years out of college an engineer may be obsolete, the same for a medical internist; five to ten years for computer technologists, ten years for

29

psychologists and eight years for authors who write on new experiments in the field of physics.'' The professor suggested that 20 percent of a person's working day should be spent keeping up-to-date. The equivalent of a day's work each week should be spent not only on learning new concepts but also on reviewing significant old ones that have been forgotten. Should not a typist be learning how to handle word processing? Should not an office manager understand the computer and data processing?

Some techniques, tactics and stratagems to consider

Many organizations will support jobholders in attending technical or professional seminars in their areas and many organizations offer internal courses that increase specific skills. We realize that insufficient time for study is often a problem, but you cannot afford to overlook opportunities to maintain, sharpen and increase your skills through such seminars and courses. And there are other elements in making your skills count that are often overlooked. Here are three strategies we recommend in assessing your skills and making them effective:

1. Learn how to explain your skills to others and in particular how to show their value. Possessing the skill may not be enough. It may be necessary that those who use it understand its full value. So ask yourself these questions: Does my job require greater skill in expressing myself? Should I learn to listen better? Do I need to take a course in some peripheral aspect of my work—understanding data processing, programming or the like?

2. Try to introduce into your work the newest usable techniques available. If someone else is using a technique in your area that has not been tried before, find out how it works from that jobholder, use it, and let your superior know you are using it and the results.

3. Acquire related skills to prepare for more interesting, more challenging and higher-grade work.

We present a self-evaluation test prepared by Julia Kearney, editor of *Manager,* a magazine published by Southwestern Bell. This test will bring to your attention the things you do best and suggest to you your managerial skills.

CHECK YOUR MANAGERIAL SKILLS

designing plans	handling a variety of projects simultaneously	working under stress	preparing a proposal
making decisions	listening to others' problems	mediating between contending parties	taking manageable risks
assigning priorities for others	solving problems	delegating	enforcing rules
breaking a complex problem into parts	paying attention to details	writing reports	
directing talents of others	teaching people new techniques	reducing expenses	thinking quickly on your feet
selling an idea or product to decision-makers	encouraging people to do better work	following up on details	composing effective letters
speaking before a group	building teamwork	specifying product standards	gathering information from many sources
negotiating to reach an understanding	tracing problems to their source	coordinating details	leading a meeting

Now take these four easy steps:

Step 1. List below five or more managerial activities you handled that you consider successes. These should be complex activities such as organizing a successful conference or getting a new program approved.

Step 2. Now, think of all the things you did to make each event successful. Use the skills listed on the left as a starting point. When you come to a skill you used to accomplish the activity, put a check mark on it. (You may want to add skills that are not listed.) In most cases, you'll find you used a number of skills for each accomplishment, so check as many as you used. Do this for each activity listed in Step 1.

Step 3. After you've analyzed your successes, list below or on another piece of paper in descending order those skills you checked the most times. These are likely the skills that you're strong in, and they're probably the ones that spur you to excellent performance.

Step 4. Based on the list above, you should have a pretty good idea of your strengths. Don't be surprised if they seem obvious. What you should do now is seek opportunities on the job to use these particular skills. If you're like most people, the more you use these skills, the more enjoyment you'll get from your job. Since people grow on the job continuously, you might redo this skills test annually.

Getting in on Time

Our economy is a time-dominated world. Productivity has a time factor. Pay has a time factor. But more basic even than these very basic economic factors, time has a meaning that speaks loud and clear in an organization. It tells the organization whether you care or not.

"Harry," Joe Carter, the personnel vice-president, said, "why can't Brent Coleman get in on time? I know he's a valuable man. We've been over that before. He works late and all that, but it just looks bad his coming in late almost every morning. It causes a morale problem. I've had complaints."

Harry Bowles, the engineering superintendent, sighed.

"Joe," Harry said at last, "I want you to think this through carefully, because if I talk to Brent, he'll leave, and you and I have got to decide whether we want a valuable engineer who gets in late or a few complaints. If the morale of the division depends on Brent's getting in on time, then I'd say we're in bad trouble."

The above scene has been recounted in several versions by our advisers. They were emphasizing the deep-seated, almost compulsive need for time discipline in an organization, a need that seems to go even beyond economic necessity. There have been efforts recently to take a more pragmatic view of the getting-in-on-time problem. Our changing life-styles have introduced some alternatives to the nine to five, forty-hour workweek, among them flexitime, permanent part-time and the compressed workweek. We shall discuss these under "Reasonable Hours and Time Management." However, whatever the time schedules an organization sets, it is important that the meaning of time in that organization be thoroughly understood. The truth is that getting in on time, whatever that time is, is important to the jobholder, even when not to the job. Edward T. Hall in his fascinating work *The Silent Language* begins his chapter "The Voices of Time" as follows: "Time talks. It speaks more plainly than words. The message it conveys comes through loud and clear. Because it is manipulated less consciously, it is subject to less distortion than the spoken language. It can shout the truth where words lie . . ."

In some societies, an hour or so late has no special import. In ours, keeping a person waiting even fifteen or twenty minutes may be considered an insult. Time, of course, has an economic impact in an organization, but even when in some special case it does not, it has a meaning. Our advisers suggest you find out what time means in your organization, not just economically but also in the culture of your company.

1. Learn the meaning of time in your company, not just in keeping the hours but also in keeping appointments, in conferences, in lunch hours and other time-dominated areas (see "Reasonable Hours and Time Management").

2. Learn the meaning of time on deadlines (see "Deadlines").

3. Learn how to manage your own time (see "Reasonable Hours and Time Management").

Reasonable Hours and Time Management

"Nine to Five" is the name of a song. "The six o'clock whistle never blew" is a line in another song. These songs, one new, one old, sum up our work time. Eight hours a day, five days a week—these have become the contemporary norms. These are considered reasonable in most organizations. There are significant exceptions. Besides the part-timer and the new "shared-job" experiments, there is the case of the entrepreneur, the young accountant in a large accounting firm, the young lawyer in the large law firm, certain professionals and the ambitious middle manager. In these categories, the five o'clock whistle never blows.

Listen to these voices:

I remember how it started. We assembled the first switch from ordinary components in our garage—my wife, my son, then ten years old, and I. That was eleven years ago. Now we have a thriving $10-million business, but I haven't had one day off or put in fewer than sixty hours a week since. And my wife and I are separated. I was never home. A business eats up your life, but I guess I wouldn't ever be able to give it up . . .

Or this:

We open at seven. We close at ten. A corner store like this serves a neighborhood. We have to stay open. People here depend on us. I guess you could say we're a mom-and-pop store, but we have to stock what they want here and we have to stay open to serve these people. That's what we have that the big department and supermarket stores don't have—personal service. We know our customers and they know us. Maybe we're a dying breed. But that's the way this business was built. We stay open. We work long hours. I doubt if I've gotten more than four hours sleep a night for the last fourteen years. And my wife too. That's the way it goes . . .

Or this:

When I started working for this firm, they told me it would be long hours in the beginning, but I never

thought I'd be working holidays and New Year's Eve
on a closing of the books like this . . .

Entrepreneurs, professionals, ambitious managers—there
is no five o'clock whistle blowing for them. But for the great
majority of us who work in organizations, the nine-to-five,
forty-hour week is still standard, though today some 20 million of us, including office workers, are now on alternate work
schedules from flexitime to concentrated workweeks of fewer
than five days. With flexitime, or flexible working hours, people are allowed to choose their starting and quitting time
within management limits. Concentrated or compressed time
schedules permit jobholders to work a three-day week with
twelve-hour days. For example, AT&T offers the compressed
workweek (three 12.5-hour days or nights per week) in
twenty-five to thirty computer centers and has found that jobs
at these centers are much sought after.

Jobholders in our society are offered reasonable hours.
Whether they keep them is another matter. There are those
who get in early and stay late. There are those who become
workaholics. Work like love can become an obsession. In our
work-oriented society this is more common than the opposite,
goofing off. The organization will tell you what it considers
reasonable hours. You will have to learn to use the reasonable
hours effectively, and that means you will have to learn to
manage your work time.

Techniques in managing your work time

Time is a major resource in the work world, and you have
only so much of it in any job. Furthermore, the higher you go
in your career and the more complex and challenging the job
becomes, the more you will need to learn how to manage your
time. Few people realize how badly, how haphazardly they

manage the time allotted to them, even when it is reasonable time.

"I can't get anything done," the harried executive says. "There're just so many hours in the day, and I just can't seem to catch up!"

"I'm working as hard as I can," Jim Knowlton says, "and yet I can't seem to finish the job, while Pete Moss over there seems to sit around doing very little and yet he gets everything done. How does he do it?"

There are many books on time management, such as R. Alec Mackenzie's *The Time Trap—How to Get More Done in Less Time,* and we recommend that you look at some of them. The principles are the same. Here are a few of them:

1. Plan your day.

2. Set objectives—what specific things are to be accomplished each day.

3. Set priorities. Determine what must be done to complete the job in contrast to what is thrust on you, what other claims there are on you or what comes up.

4. Be ruthless in protecting your priorities and your time plan. Learn to say no skillfully and without causing resentment.

5. Learn to delegate.

R. Alec Mackenzie, the consultant on time management, has worked out this list of time wasters, their possible causes and possible solutions:

TIME WASTER	POSSIBLE CAUSES	SOLUTIONS
Lack of planning	Failure to see the benefit	Recognize that planning takes time but saves time in the end.
	Action orientation	Emphasize results, not activity.

37

TIME WASTER	POSSIBLE CAUSES	SOLUTIONS
	Success without it	Recognize that success is often in spite of, not because of, methods.
Lack of priorities	Lack of goals and objectives	Write down goals and objectives. Discuss priorities with subordinates.
Overcommitment	Broad interests	Say no.
	Confusion in priorities	Put first things first.
	Failure to set priorities	Develop a personal philosophy of time. Relate priorities to a schedule of events.
Management by crisis	Lack of planning	Apply the same solutions as for lack of planning.
	Unrealistic time estimates	Allow more time. Allow for interruptions.
	Problem orientation	Be opportunity-oriented.
	Reluctance of subordinates to break bad news	Encourage fast transmission of information as essential for timely corrective action.
Haste	Impatience with detail	Take time to get it right. Save the time of doing it over.
	Responding to the urgent	Distinguish between the urgent and the important.
	Lack of planning ahead	Take time to plan. It repays itself many times over.
	Attempting too much in too little time	Attempt less. Delegate more.
Paperwork and reading	Knowledge explosion	Read selectively. Learn speed reading.

TIME WASTER	POSSIBLE CAUSES	SOLUTIONS
	Computeritis	Manage computer data by exception.
	Failure to screen	Remember the Pareto principle. Delegate reading to subordinates.
Routine and trivia	Lack of priorities	Set and concentrate on goals. Delegate nonessentials.
	Oversurveillance of subordinates	Delegate; then give subordinates their head. Look to results, not details or methods.
	Refusal to delegate; feeling of greater security dealing with operating detail	Recognize that without delegation it is impossible to get anything done through others.
Visitors	Enjoyment of socializing	Do it elsewhere. Meet visitors outside. Suggest lunch if necessary. Hold stand-up conferences.
	Inability to say no	Screen. Say no. Be unavailable. Modify the open-door policy.
Telephone	Lack of self-discipline	Screen and group calls. Be brief.
	Desire to be informed and involved	Stay uninvolved with all but essentials. Manage by exception.
Meetings	Fear of responsibility for decisions	Make decisions without meetings.
	Indecision	Make decisions even when some facts are missing.
	Overcommunication	Discourage unnecessary meetings. Convene only those needed.

TIME WASTER	POSSIBLE CAUSES	SOLUTIONS
	Poor leadership	Use agendas. Stick to the subject. Prepare concise minutes as soon as possible.
Indecision	Lack of confidence in the facts	Improve fact-finding and validating procedures.
	Insistence on all the facts—paralysis of analysis	Accept risks as inevitable. Decide without all facts.
	Fear of the consequences of a mistake	Delegate the right to be wrong. Use mistakes as a learning process.
	Lack of a rational decision-making process	Get facts, set goals, investigate alternatives and negative consequences, make the decision, and implement it.
Lack of delegation	Fear of subordinates' inadequacy	Train. Allow mistakes. Replace if necessary.
	Fear of subordinates' competence	Delegate fully. Give credit. Ensure corporate growth to maintain challenge.
	Work overload on subordinates	Balance the workload. Staff up. Reorder priorities.

*The list is adapted from "Troubleshooting Chart for Time-Wasters," in R. Alec Mackenzie, *Managing Time at the Top* (New York: The Presidents Association, 1970).

Finally:

1. Keep reasonable hours.
2. Do not become a workaholic (see "Killing Yourself").

Being Efficient

"The man's a wonder," Cliff said to the consultant. "He gets out some two hundred of these summary reports a month, all on time, going to twenty departments, some seven hundred people. He's been churning them out for us for three years now. They're correct, neat, the right information and, best of all, on time. Since he took over the data processing, production has increased and we've had no screw-ups."

"That's very interesting," the consultant said. "Who initiates these reports?"

"At one time or another, various departments asked for them. They're in a format Harry devised. Harry has all the data on that."

"I gather that some two thousand four hundred of these summary reports go out every year to various departments or a total of about nine thousand copies of these reports, some ten or fifteen pages long, each year."

"Yes, Harry has a report on that too. He puts out his own report on how efficient his department is. Harry's a wonder. You should have seen the mess before he took over. Wrong data, inaccuracies, reports coming out late."

Later the consultant sat in front of Harry's desk. Harry, an earnest, corpulent, middle-aged man, his mind elsewhere, was being polite.

"No, I don't know why some of these reports are needed," he said. He looked at the consultant. He was a bit nettled. "If an authorized person asks for this report, he gets it. That's my job."

Harry is efficient.

Harry does the work—planning, organizing, and running it with a minimum of waste and within the time frame required.

However, the question arises: Is being efficient enough?

41

Let us look at another example of efficiency quoted by a supervisor: "It's a bureaucracy we've got here," Glen Rider said. "They're efficient as hell—but to what purpose? The place goes like clockwork. You fill out the form. The form is processed immediately. A record is made in triplicate. The shipment goes out and we lose three dollars on every order filled. What's happening is we're efficient in losing money . . ."

As one of our advisers pointed out, efficiency itself is not enough. Doing it right is not enough. The critical management function, as Peter Drucker has written, is not to do things right but to do the right things. The objective must always be kept in mind.

Questions to ask yourself about your own efficiency

1. What is the measure of efficiency in your job?

2. Are the various measures of efficiency—reports per month, transactions per day—realistic within the context of the whole enterprise?

3. Do these measures lead to effectiveness or simply to spinning wheels or less-than-useful results?

4. Does the work you have planned, organized, administered and controlled lead to both efficiency and effectiveness (see "Who Depends on Me?")?

Being Effective

"When I was young," one of our advisers said, "I had a certain expertise that one of the biggest companies in that new field was seeking. My father had been a friend of the chairman of the huge organization. The chairman was a man famed in the business world as being a tyrant and a power broker, a mover and shaker, and I had no desire to leave the small firm where I worked to become part of this corporate behemoth. My father, however, was proud of his friendship with the chairman and had misguidedly set up an appointment for me to see him. I went so as not to disappoint my father.

"I arrived at two-thirty in the afternoon, the appointed time, at the elaborate corporate headquarters and went to the sixtieth floor to the chairman's anteroom. I was quite nervous though I did not want any job they could offer, but the public image of this man was ferocious, and I expected he would brush me off quickly when he saw how young I was and that I lacked enthusiasm.

"His secretary graciously told me he was expecting me. I had heard stories of how people trembled in his presence, how a word from him toppled careers and sent shivers through the industry. And yet, of course, he was also revered and had been considered one of the greatest salesmen and marketers of the complex hardware of my field.

" 'Mr. Arrow would like to see you now, Mr. Connolly,' the secretary said.

"I entered a palatial office.

"The man who rose from the huge desk to come forward to greet me was tall and slim with a rather shy and diffident smile. He came to me and grasped my hand in both of his as if he had been looking forward to seeing me for a long time.

" 'How kind of you to come,' he said to me. 'I know how busy you must be. Your father is justly proud of you.' "

"I was twenty-eight years old. This man was in his sixties, one of the business world's most powerful and influential figures; yet he treated me that afternoon not just as an equal but as if I were doing him a great favor by coming to see him. He took me to one of the sofas near the windows overlooking the Manhattan skyline and the river, and he sat opposite me in an easy chair as if he had all the time in the world, and we talked mostly about me, my life and my world.

"I have worked for that giant organization that I did not want to join for twenty years now. I still remember this man who could not repress his enthusiasm for me and, as I learned later, for anyone he needed or wanted or who interested him, and I have understood since the source of this man's power. He has retired since but he is the most effective man I have ever met."

Key considerations in being effective

1. Being effective means being able to get the most desirable results.

2. Being effective may have less to do with your efficiency as measured by efficiency standards than with your ability to see which of the many objectives of what you are doing will bring the best results.

3. Being effective may also mean your ability to reach people who can help you achieve the best objective.

4. Setting the right objective and meeting it is being effective.

Bringing the Home into the Office

"He's like a bear today," the secretary remarked. "His wife must have let him have it. I hope Guy Fenton calls him in. He'll unload on Guy, and Guy won't put up with it. The man's homelife is a disaster, and we're the ones who suffer."

"Yeah," the administrative vice-president's executive secretary answered, "and next time he asks you

44

to pick up something for his wife's birthday or help him arrange his daughter's party, tell him that's not what they told you was going to be part of this job. Working for this turkey is like being present at a specially disorganized family squabble. You have your own husband and children, you don't need his family life too.''

Or take the case of Jimbo Bates:

"I have to take an extra hour at noon, Tom," Jimbo is saying to his manager. "The kid really needs to have his eyes looked at and Janet has to see her mother again. The old lady's always bitchin' about being neglected. So I know I been a little irregular lately, Tom, but you know how it is—families. They're a pain in the ass sometimes.''

"Jimbo," Tom replies tiredly, "you've either been late or had errands to do or left early for the last three months. Now as you say, I know how families are—I got one myself—but they're paying us for an eight-hour day. If we all did this, the place would be a shambles. Marilyn there has two kids to take care of and no husband now but she's here on time and she doesn't take an hour or so off here and there. If it's a real emergency, sure that's different. But getting the kid's teeth fixed, leaving early to pick up a package for Janet, taking an hour off for this and that of your family obligations. . . . Jimbo, we all have our troubles and families, and they can be very demanding, but you're bringing your home into the office and it ain't fair to the rest of us. Now take off this hour and don't be asking me for any more of the company's time unless it's a real emergency.''

The difficulties of holding a job and raising a family have

increased in recent years largely because of the two-paycheck family, where both the husband and wife have jobs and are at the same time trying to raise children. The problem has been met to some extent by alternate or part-time job schedules, but intrusions like that of the executive who brings company personnel into his homelife or like Jimbo Bates who in a sense brings his home into the office are a nuisance in the work world and an irritant to their associates.

Our advisers have commented that changing life-styles have loosened the hard line that once existed between work and homelife. They also have pointed out that this is a two-way street. There are many professionals and executives who bring the work world into their homelife and cause their families irritation and hardship. Nevertheless, they agreed a person must plan so that these worlds do not encroach on the time one owes either to his or her work or to the home and family. To paraphrase in a less exalted key a famous phrase: Render unto the company that which is the company's and unto the home that which is the home's.

Techniques, tactics and stratagems in managing both a career and a family

There is no simple prescription for this common and sometimes agonizing dilemma. You can only plan and compromise. But feeling guilty about a problem of this magnitude that cannot be ideally solved is a waste of time and life. Work out some plan that your family will agree to and then stick to it.

Managing both a home and a career means:

1. *Planning* so that there is time apportioned to each, even if this requires compromise in both areas.
2. Not bringing family matters into the workplace.
3. Not allowing your work and your career to overwhelm your family life.

Killing Yourself

Jim Keeler gets into the office at eight and rarely leaves before seven-thirty in the evening, sometimes staying until ten or eleven. Ordinarily he catches the 8:05 to Greenwich, where he lives with his wife and children. Everyone tells him he is working too hard. He is killing himself. He has gone up fast in the company. He gets things done and he expects those who report to him to be in early and get the work out fast and stay late if necessary.

At home his wife is a busy woman also, bringing up the kids, running the big house, attending PTA meetings, participating in community activities. The children are very busy— they have fast-track activities. They are picked up by the school bus each weekday morning to go to an expensive private school. They have a school life filled with extracurricular activities. They are rarely bored but often tired and anxious.

Jim has a middle manager's job that can lead to bigger things, and there are a lot of ways to handle it. His predecessor was a relaxed, easygoing office politician who was not noted for extending himself, and when Jim came in, it was like a breath of fresh air. He took over and things began to hum. The office politician is Jim's boss. He appreciates what Jim is doing. He got where he is, he tells people, by picking people like Jim who are smarter and harder working than he is.

But Jim has a problem. At his annual medical checkup, the doctor tells him his blood pressure is too high for a man of his age and there are heart murmurs. He is, the doctor tells him, the famous Type A personality, bucking for the coronary, unless he can slow down a little. He has got to learn to take it a little easier.

"Sure, sure," Jim says, but aside from getting in five minutes later and going home five minutes earlier for the first couple of weeks after the checkup, he is back to his old routine and he doesn't know how to go about taking it easier. He doesn't know what taking it easy means. He hates vacations and holidays. A two-week vacation is torture to him. He gets restless and usually gets sick. He has found if he takes enough work with him, he can get through his annual vacation without the restlessness, symptoms of anxiety and cold sweats that would otherwise assail him. He feels a vacation longer than two weeks would kill him. He is, in short, a workaholic.

The compulsive nature of a psychological dependence on work has been described in psychiatric journals and it appears to have become more common in our work-oriented society. In his book *Work and Love*, Dr. J. B. Rohrlick describes some typical symptoms of the workaholic:

> Work can be just as strong a narcotic as heroin in terms of its mood-altering properties. . . . When a person must work while sleeping or instead of sleeping, while eating, while making love or reading a novel, while talking to friends or playing with his children, while swimming, sipping wine or taking a walk through the autumn woods, he is revealing what he *cannot* do. The work addict has no choice in the matter, even when he wants to change. *He cannot stop working*. His life is defined by his work pattern. All other activities and relationships are secondary. . . . We may also infer the presence of work addiction from the appearance of medical illness as a direct result of overwork. This, of course, is much easier to ascertain when we are dealing with addiction to toxic substances, such as alcohol, which cause predictable changes in such organs as the liver, the pancreas and the brain. But, oddly enough, many work addicts are large consumers of such drugs as alcohol and marijuana, because they are the only means by which they can wrench themselves away from their compulsive work orientation. And while many addicts who launch themselves into physical-fitness regimens with a determined working additude, there are others who neglect their health because of their obsessive concentration on their jobs. They begin to show signs of physical deterioration. They may smoke sev-

eral packs of cigarets a day, drink too much or become overweight from eating too much. . . . Lack of sleep may catch up with them physically, and accidents may occur with greater frequency, leading to serious injury.

The workaholic has been pictured as a figure of fun in our society, but this can be a serious problem, both for you, if you become a workaholic and for anyone who works for you. Our advisers hope you never have to report to a workaholic.

If you have a combination of the following symptoms, it may be time to seek help:

1. Your life is completely defined by your work pattern. All other activities are secondary.
2. You seem to have withdrawal symptoms if you are away from your work routines even for a short period: intense anxiety, a feeling of helplessness and disorientation, feelings of guilt, sleeplessness, loss of appetite.
3. Illnesses that appear during vacations or when away from work.
4. Illnesses associated with overwork: nervous tension, heavy smoking and drinking to keep going.
5. Neglect of family and friends and normal relationships because of work habits.

Goofing Off

John Halliday awoke that morning and knew his life was over. It was his fortieth birthday, and just that week he had been told he was not going to get the managership in Duluth. He had worked hard for it. He had put in some eighty-hour weeks during the last year. He realized he was in competition with some other very hot executives, but he had thought he had a good chance. Now he realized he had come to a midlife crisis, and this loss indicated to him that he had reached the end of the line. He was through. He was stuck here in the same old job, in the same old routine, and it seemed to him that this was his life. He would never get any further. He had reached the plateau.

There has been a lot of talk about "plateauing out" in the middle-management work world, as if finding a job that fulfills a person's abilities and requirements were nothing but a way station to something better. A career may mandate that you remain generally in one area of the corporate world, that your particular abilities and proclivities are best used and best fulfilled at a level you find acceptable. What happened to John Halliday, however, was hope deferred, and as the Bible says, "Hope deferred maketh the heart grow sick." The result: He decided to goof off, to not try anymore, to just settle in and do as little as possible. They would never get him to lift a finger for anything again. This type of goofing off, when one has been deeply disappointed by a rejection, when ambition has been destroyed can be serious, serious to the jobholder's status and to his or her usefulness to the organization but even more serious for the person. The flavor goes out of the fruit, the tang goes out of life. The person can be destroyed.

Now let us look at the case of Barry Leland, also disappointed in the job:

> "This job is going nowhere, Steve," Barry tells his best friend, "and I'm going nowhere with it. It's boring. The same old thing day after day, the same old faces, the same chickenshit complaining and conniving. And for what? There must be something better in life. I'm taking it easy from now on. I'm tuning out."
>
> "Well, Barry," Steve says, "you used to like it in the beginning. Work's work, you know. Where does it say it has to be interesting? It just has to be done. You can goof off, if you want, but that isn't going to make it any more interesting. It's going to make it even more boring. You're just having a bad day."

Our advisers sympathized with these people. It happens at times to all of us, they remarked. In the case of the midlife crisis, however, they suggested John Halliday get help to get through this period. Objectively, they felt his career was far from over, that he would live to fight another day, but the trauma of working hard for something finally denied him, of ambition thwarted, can be serious, and he could use help from professionals or friends or his wife. For Barry, they had less sympathy. If the job is boring, perhaps he should look around for a better one. If it is only a temporary bad period, don't worry about it. We all have the blahs, they said. You'll get over it. Goofing off is rarely the answer.

Things to consider in handling a period of goofing off

1. You cannot work at the same pitch over any great period of time.
2. Goofing off once in a while may be beneficial.
3. Goofing off for a long period or permanently through disappointment or despair is self-destructive.
4. Goofing off because of boredom only increases the boredom (see "Boredom").
5. Goofing off is a symptom. Find out why you are doing it. If it is because of boredom or despair, take measures.

Who's the Best Worker?

In every organization and group there is always someone who is relaxed and cheerful, who never seems rushed or strained, and yet seems to get everything done with consummate ease. You look at this person and then at your own shambles of a day, the work endlessly piling up, the things that should have been done yesterday, the dollar-short and day-late syndrome. How does this paragon in your group, who has just as much work as you, perhaps more, do it?

You will usually find, our advisers tell us, that these tremendous workers have learned two secrets: they know how to manage one of their most irreplaceable assets—time—and they know how to delegate.

The management of time may be an art (see "Reasonable Hours and Time Management"), but there are two specific tricks that can help make your days more productive. We have recommended that you read books on time management and have listed one or two in the "Suggested Readings" section in the Appendix, but we would like to mention here the most important of all the time-management devices: the list. What, you ask yourself each morning, are the two or three or four things that, if you do them today, will make you feel you have done a day's work? You simply jot them down, and whatever else you do that day, even if you do nothing else, you do them.

This has been tried and found most useful. The best workers usually have that list. If your day is spent putting out fires, so to speak—and many people have nothing but days like that—you may end up feeling you have done nothing but stay alive. Staying alive is important, but each day you want to do more than that. You want to have done two or three things that add to the sum of your existence. The list will help you do this.

The second secret of the best worker is that he or she delegates. One of our consultants has defined an executive as a person who takes all the credit, avoids all the work and passes on all the blame. One of our executives has countered by defining a consultant as a man who knows 101 ways to make love but he doesn't know any girls. But buried in the rather heavy humor of our business world is the meaning of the word *delegate*. The tremendous worker knows who and how much and what kind of work should be done by others in order to complete his own job. He knows how to get cooperation, how to inspire and how to assess capacities and how to give credit. Again and again you hear from the outstanding executives a ringing of the changes on "I learned to find people smarter than myself to help do the work. Sometimes I may end up working for them, but they never forget I gave them their start and they always make me look good."

Measuring Yourself

In a job, learn to quantify. Learn to put numbers to your work. You will be surprised at the insight this may give you. How much, how many, how often? If you are a grocery clerk, how many trips do you make in a day, how many bags do you carry? If you are a professor of classical languages, how many words from Latin are used in everyday English, how many students took classical languages this year compared with ten years ago?

Pythagoras taught that the universe was ruled by number, and number gives many insights. All mammals, as Stephen Jay Gould, the Harvard paleontologist, noted, have their lives numbered in breaths and heartbeats. And measured in this way, all animals have the same life-span, an average of 200 million breaths and 800 million heartbeats, small animals living fast, their 200 million breaths consumed in a few years, large animals living slower and longer by our time, but only man living three times as long as he should.

In the work world, measurement and number can enable you to increase the efficiency and effectiveness of your work. It can even give you an insight into the value of your work. There are four kinds of measurement commonly used in the work world. The first is accounting, which gives you the *cost* of the work, usually in dollars. The second is production, which gives you the *quantity*. The third is inspection or testing which gives you the *quality* of the work, and the fourth is the *time* measurement which in time study measures the time it takes to produce a certain quantity of work of a specified quality.

Managers use these four measures in most management

work for planning, organizing, administering and controlling. Even representative management work has been measured.

Some years ago Philip Marvin of the University of Cincinnati made a survey for the American Management Association of how representative executives spent their workday. His representative group was made up of some thirteen hundred executives at all levels and in all parts of the country. Regardless of the level or kind of company, their work habits were surprisingly consistent. The survey found that 47 percent of their daily work time was spent in purely management functions (planning, organizing, administering and controlling); 31 percent of their daily time in the functional role of their skills (accounting, if they were accountants, selling or marketing if they were in those fields, engineering or technical work if from those areas); 16 percent of their time in their mentor role, teaching or showing others how to do things or helping others solve problems. The professor did not specify what happened to the other 6 percent of their generally very long workday. Perhaps it was spent goofing off.

But the measurements went beyond that. In breaking down the management role, which took up about half the time of the workday, the survey showed that making decisions took up 19 percent of the manager's time, planning 19 percent, organizing (that is, defining who does what and who is accountable to whom) 13 percent, delegating 12 percent, staffing 7 percent, evaluating 8 percent and controlling (comparing with norms or expectations and correcting) 12 percent of the executive's time. Finally, innovating, trying something new or a new direction, took 10 percent of the person's time. Thus, even managing can be somewhat measured in terms of type of activities performed during the workday.

Measure yourself. Learn to quantify. In the work world as in life, two of your most important and useful skills will be language and quantification, words and numbers. Perhaps it is worth knowing that you have maybe 200 million heartbeats to go.

Techniques, tactics and stratagems in learning to be productive

1. Take your work apart and measure it.

2. Quantify your productivity.

3. Quantify insofar as possible your value to the company in terms of such measurable factors as number of inquiries, orders, sales, presentations, items produced and, if possible, amount of income or profit through your activities.

4. Set production standards for yourself and better them.

5. Develop yourself as an executive. Most organizations have continuing education or executive-development courses for their people to keep them abreast of new developments in the world in which the organization operates. Take advantage of these courses. Here are two examples of managerial courses offered jobholders by one large organization:

Examples of Management Development Courses

Name of Course: Managerial Effectiveness

WHO SHOULD ATTEND?

Middle and senior-level managers who have demonstrated management proficiency and talent.

OBJECTIVE

To maximize a manager's effectiveness by developing a personal management style. Individual achievement of this objective will not be measured on a "right/wrong" index.

SUBJECTS COVERED

A. Self-analysis
    • Understanding and improving your areas of strength

- How you see yourself and others
- Interaction with others

B. Improving Working Relationships with the Organization
    - The accomplishment of "work" by individuals
    - The relationship of the individual to the team
    - The relationship of teams to the total organization

C. Improving Interpersonal Relations
    - How to enhance communication skills and techniques
    - Recognizing your own communication style and that of others

D. Building/Creating a Personal Management Style
    - Alternatives in managerial action
    - Situational management
    - Selecting what works best for you

LENGTH: A 3½-day workshop

The profession of management

WHO SHOULD ATTEND?

Experienced middle- and upper-level managers and those recently promoted to such positions. Particularly for managers who supervise professional staff.

OBJECTIVE

To provide a clear understanding of "management work" for the person who must get work done through other managers. Participants will:

- gain a better insight into management functions—planning, organizing, leading and controlling.
- identify personal management skills that need upgrading and develop a plan for improvement.

LENGTH: A 4-day seminar

Anxiety

"I don't think I'm going to be able to take it anymore," John Helmut said. "The place seems to be falling apart, and I'm really disappointed in Larry. I thought he'd show more common sense and insight into what's going on."

"What's the matter, dear?" his wife Carole asked. It was an autumn evening. John had come in on the 7:02, late and tired.

"Larry's given this new man the assignment on the Barrington account."

"But I thought you didn't want that account," his wife said. "You told me that might be the straw that broke the camel's back."

"That's true, Carole," John said, "but to give it to this new man, Rich Field, who's not really been tried out yet, a big important account like that—I don't think he can handle it."

"Well, I guess we'll just have to wait and see," Carole said. "Whom else could he give it to?"

"Well, I'd rather take it over myself than trust someone who hasn't yet won his spurs. And Larry didn't even have the courtesy to ask my advice."

"I thought you liked Larry," Carole said. "You told me he was the best boss you'd had yet . . ."

"Well, I'm not so sure of his judgment now."

What tangled motivations and insecurities lie hidden in the above conversation. And underneath them all lies that inescapable emotion that arises at times in every job—anxiety. No jobholder can fully escape it. You will feel it and your boss will feel it—it goes with the territory, and you may as well face it and understand the reason for it, at least the most basic of the reasons.

The most basic reason for anxiety in any job is simple. It arises from the dependency relationship. Wherever there is a dependency relationship, no matter how fruitful and good it is otherwise, there will be anxiety and a love-hate emotion. You as a jobholder are dependent on your job, so you will have an ambivalent feeling, a love-hate feeling from time to time for the organization, for your boss and sometimes even for your peers and subordinates. As John Wareham, the international executive recruiter, remarked in this connection, referring to the old song, "Frankie didn't kill Johnny because he was cheating on her but because she depended on him for love." Being dependent creates repressed anger and thus anxiety.

Oddly enough, your boss and the organization, being to some degree dependent on your work, may from time to time feel this ambivalence and anxiety about you. Of course, you know and we all know that no one is indispensable and as long as this is the case, we will all at times suffer from anxiety.

Techniques, tactics and strategies to deal with anxiety

When you are attacked by anxiety, here are three strategies that have helped others:

1. Talk it out with someone you trust.
2. If it arises from the dependency relationship, seek reassurance as to your value in the company by discussing your apprehensions unemotionally with your superior.
3. Immerse yourself in outside activities. Pay attention to private matters and get a good night's sleep.

Loving the Work

Work gets better as you go along in your career, and it is habit forming. It is also indispensable to a full life.

Frederick Herzberg, the social scientist, author of a classic study of work motivation, once remarked: "The trouble with the Garden of Eden was that Adam and Eve had wonderful fringe benefits, but they had no work." It was not only the knowledge of good and evil the two blessed inhabitants of the Garden of Eden lacked but the equally important chance to define and build their lives through work.

The work ethic of our culture, which has been decried from time to time, has been a great part of mankind's uniquely human heritage. Work, defined as goal-oriented activity, is unique to human beings. No other animal truly "works" in this sense. Animals are programmed to their activities at birth to meet their adaptive needs—eating, sleeping, hunting, building nests, defending territories and other even more complex routines. They can even be taught to do man's work for him, but conceiving the goal, looking into the future and envisioning an end toward which to strive is beyond them, as is the knowledge of good and evil. We alone can conceive of a goal in the distant future, knowing also that we are destined to die, and still work toward it.

The job you have should provide you with work you love or work that fulfills your psychic needs. There are times in your life when you will work hard and the work will strain you and sometimes almost tear you apart. These are the times, however, that you will remember best. These are the times that the veterans in high positions like to talk about—"when we worked all night to meet an emergency," "when we managed to break the code," "when we kept going for thirty-six hours to get the job done . . ."

"In the sweat of thy brow," the Lord admonished Adam, "thou will labor all the days of thy life. . . ." Besides the two-edged sword of the knowledge of good and evil, that admonition has turned out to be not a punishment but the greatest blessing the Lord has given man.

Strategies in learning to love your work

1. Get some fun out of your work. Tailor your job to your psychic needs. Work should be fun if it is to be done well.

2. Treasure the times you have distinguished yourself.

3. Do not allow the "team spirit" syndrome to rob you of the true accomplishments that are due you, even if you do not boast of them or if they are not recognized by others. Glory in your achievements. They are among the greatest satisfactions of life.

Hating the Work

The worst jobs are the "warm body" jobs.

They are the jobs where you are paid for just being there—receptionist, gofer, assistant and other jobs where the activity, the real "work," is at a minimum. Many jobs in the beginning of a career are of this type.

These apprentice jobs may be boring, trivial and wasteful of your time and capacities. One of the hardest tasks in the world is looking busy when you have little or nothing to do. The days are long. Time moves like molasses. The five o'clock whistle never seems to blow.

Such early jobs occur often in the white collar and lower professional areas. They need you but not eight hours a day or five days a week. They need you maybe one or two hours on some days. The work may require only four or five hours on other days.

What do you do?

No myth is more persistent than that of the difficulty of early jobs. School is generally the hardest job a young person will have for the early part of his career. It will require more of him than any early job he will ever have. College and professional school may even prove harder than any future job. The graduate comes into what he is told is a challenging world in which he will be able to use his education. Unfortunately, he does not start as president or even as vice-president and he is disillusioned to find that his so-called apprenticeship and the job itself so glowingly described in the career brochure are not as advertised. They are neither challenging nor complex, and in some cases he could be forgiven for feeling that his ten-year-old brother could do the job easily after school and before dinner.

Challenging jobs are apparently not handed out on silver platters. You have to earn them. You have to do your time. You have to do the uninteresting, unimportant but necessary

61

scutwork. So try not to hate the work too much. Look at it carefully. Do what you have to do conscientiously. Learn everything you can about that field and about what your boss and others are doing in their jobs. Keep alive outside interests and activities.

Keep your eyes open for the next step. No one is going to make your job "interesting," despite all the talk of job enrichment during the last ten years or so. There are millions of dull jobs that are paid for. You have to make a living. They have to pay you to do those jobs but they don't have to make them interesting or challenging. You will have to do that yourself. It is hard to do if you hate the work.

It may help to remember there are better days ahead and that you can learn things not taught in school. The composing of Beethoven's Fifth may be said to have begun when he learned the scales, and one can take comfort in the famous remark made by Paderewski, the world-renowned pianist, when someone called him a genius.

"Yes," he said, "but before I was a genius, I was a drudge."

Tactics and strategies in facing a hateful job

1. Do the scutwork that is part of any job cheerfully.

2. Avoid "warm body" jobs unless you can use the time to study, read and learn.

3. Keep your eyes open for work that will stretch you and take you onward.

4. Ask for more work, if you see others can use help. Otherwise, turn to outside activities.

5. If your hatred of the job becomes chronic, look around for other work. Never waste in hating a job the most precious thing you have—your life.

Deadlines

In the work world, missing deadlines is a major crime.
Getting something in on time is important.

But there are deadlines and deadlines, and there are some things jobholders should know about getting things in on time. "I want that report on my desk by Thursday morning" is different from "Do you think you can get it in to me in a couple of weeks?" or "The Committee Report should be ready in July."

If you are bright, the report will be on the vice-president's desk Thursday morning. If you care about the project, you will get it to the manager in two weeks. If you think the committee report will be ready in July, you do not know committees.

Strategies in setting and meeting deadlines

1. Remember to put a deadline for yourself on any project of significance.

2. Remember most things take longer and cost more than estimated.

3. Never let anyone put you off with "I will do it as soon as possible." Insist on a date or a time.

4. Learn your own work rhythm. Are you one of those who do best when the deadline is upon you?

5. "We'll think about it" means never.

6. "When you get around to it" means never.

7. "There's no hurry" means never.

8. In making important decisions, wait until the last minute. You need the time to let your subconscious mind, where past experience and intuition lie, come to your aid.

Boredom

Boredom tells you something. Boredom on the job is serious. It tells you it is time to take stock. It also tells you you have two choices: shape up or move on.

First, taking stock.

You must ask yourself what makes the job boring.

The work?
The people?
You?
Your own life?
The way you are going about it?

The work

No matter how trivial or repetitious a task is, habit can make it quite pleasant on most days. Anything that is part of a routine can become habit forming, and the part of your job that you can make a part of a routine not only will be bearable but you will miss it if it is not there. For the total job, however, there must be involvement, and when you can no longer become involved in your job, boredom sets in and you must look at the job from another angle or consider looking beyond to another job.

The people

You are tired of the same old faces. You are fed up with Jim's problems with his girl friend, with Mary's stomach ulcers, with the boss's sour face on Monday mornings. What is the answer? Widen your acquaintanceship in the organization. Get to know people in other departments. Have lunch with somebody else. Have lunch with someone in your kind of job in another company. Look at others. Perhaps you had better take a look at yourself also.

You

Maybe you have become boring. Look at yourself. How do you come across to others? Are you too self-centered? Are you able to be interested only in things that have to do with you and your welfare? Are you too absorbed in getting on, in self-gratification, in self-aggrandizement? Most of us are. We become bored with ourselves even, and then we are bored with everything else. And we ourselves are boring. Get out of yourself. Forget yourself and get interested in someone or something else.

Your own life

You may be going through a period when you need help. You may have lost your sense of direction. If you are at the so-called midlife crisis, you may feel that you took the wrong turn some years ago and you are now at a dead end. Talk it out with someone you can trust: your wife or husband, your best friend or a professional, a psychiatrist or psycho-analyst. Should you consider a new direction? Should you look for an old dream? Boredom is a symptom. Pay attention to it.

The way you are going about it

You may have come to feel the job has no more possibilities and the way you are handling it is the only way it can or should be handled. The challenge is gone, the pleasure is gone. Your first move is to go to your boss or to others with expertise in your area and to people who have had your job before and ask their opinion of the way you are handling it and how it might be improved. You may be surprised to find there are aspects of your job you have overlooked. You may learn something new about handling your job that can awaken your interest in its possibilities.

Strategies in facing up to and overcoming boredom

Your second step after taking stock is to decide whether you should or can move on. Every job has periods of boredom, and they pass. But if the condition continues and becomes chronic, you must take it seriously. Boredom is a killer. It has killed many a promising jobholder. It can kill you. You become lethargic. You lose your zest for life. You die before your time. If nothing helps and the nature of the job and of the life it imposes on you cannot be changed, then you must consider moving on. Turn to Part IV, "The Outside Work World," and consider the alternatives.

Who Depends on Me?

No job in an organization can be done alone. All jobs involve other people, and whether these people report to you or are simply associates or you report to them, you will depend on them and they will depend on you. Therefore, you will need to "manage" your work so that you get their cooperation and they get yours.

What does managing mean?

Managing is made up of five basic elements: Planning, communicating, organizing, administering and controlling.

Planning
No matter what your job is, plan it carefully so that it fits into the overall enterprise. If your job has been planned by others, look at the plan carefully and expand it or modify it to suit your mode and style of work and its contribution to the enterprise.

Communicating
To make any plan work, it must be communicated clearly and persuasively to those whom it affects. To get cooperation, you must let those whom you need know about your job or project and its value and the part you hope they will play in it.

You must also inspire and make it worthwhile for them to play that part.

Organizing

The job must be organized in such a way that you and those who contribute to it can operate effectively. Schedules, times, amounts, sequences, assignments, contributions—these must all be arranged so as to make the job understandable and relatively easy to complete. If it is a complex job, responsibilities and authorities must be worked out rationally and properly assigned.

Administering

This means you must be on top of the job, either carrying out the functions assigned to yourself or directing or assisting others for whose work you are responsible.

Controlling

At each step of the way you must check the results to see that the work meets the plan, standards or specifications and then make whatever adjustments are necessary.

That, in short, is called managing and managing is the major skill you will need to develop as you move into more and more complex jobs and particularly into work that involves others and gives you authority over them.

Getting Transferred

At a certain level in most organizations, the chances of being transferred to some other part of the organization and having to move may become part of the career path. In any event, the possibilities of being transferred in our mobile and widespread economic world are always present in a career, particularly in a large and far-flung organization, and the dilemma presented by such a transfer can be traumatic.

"Jim," Harold Jennings began on that Tuesday morning, as Jim Hartzell seated himself in his boss's office, "I have what I hope is a pleasant surprise for you. Ken Marsden is being moved to take over the St. Louis operations, and you have been chosen to take his place in Houston. This, of course, is a promotion, but it means a move for you and I would like to discuss the possibilities with you and ask you to consider the job with all its promise . . ."

"Ellen," John Hanrahan said, as Ellen Cord seated herself in his office, "I know you've probably heard rumors about our operation being moved to Hartford. Well, the orders have come down officially and I hope I can count on you to come with us . . ."

These scenes represent the two most common situations in getting transferred. Jim Hartzell is being promoted, and this may be the first of two or three transfers in his career path. In the second case, the operations of that group are being moved to another location and chances are there will be no job for Ellen if she is unwilling to move with them.

In any event, both situations are traumatic, since they may involve families, children in school and a new life-style. In situations where both husband and wife have jobs, it is no longer axiomatic that the man's job and career should take precedence, and the dilemma becomes agonizing. In any case, where you have a family, others in your family are being asked to be uprooted and to refashion their lives for your career.

Key factors to consider in a transfer

There are seven factors you must consider and resolve when confronted with these situations:

First, you must consider what the consequences would be if you decide not to move. Will your career be over in that organization? Will it simply be delayed? Will it mean that you can continue but that you are shut off from certain positions or from the level of responsibility you have aspired to? These questions should be thoroughly worked out in your own mind and discussed with your family. In addition to the career consequences, you must try to work out the economic consequences both pro and con and how they could affect your family's future.

Second, you must explore whether this is to be the last transfer or whether you would be coming back to headquarters later or to the office from which you are being transferred and, if possible, what the time frame affecting such transfers might be—two years? Five years? Ten years?

Third, you must explore thoroughly with your boss what this means to your future, what the company will do for you, how much help the company will give you in moving and getting settled and generally what life-style the company's compensation will allow you in the new community.

Fourth, you should ask for as much time as possible to talk it over with your family and to consider all its implications. You may have only one or two weeks before a decision is required.

Fifth, you will want to learn everything you can about the new community you are being transferred to. You should, if possible, visit the new location before making your decision and talk to associates who have been there or are living there now.

Sixth, taking into account all the implications of the transfer, this is a good time to sit down and once more analyze your career goals, your overall life priorities, such as community service activities, hobbies, interests, and environmental needs to determine the future effects of the move on your family and your life.

Finally, if you decide to accept the transfer, accept it wholeheartedly and make the most of the advantages it can bring you and your family.

In recent years, with the increase in communications and mobility, many organizations have managed to cut down the frequency of transfers of executives. Nevertheless, as you advance in you career, you must be aware that transfers become a possibility.

Other Jobs

People in an organization often try to protect their jobs from others, that is, they do not want you or anyone else to "help" them or to enter what they consider their territory.

"I'd appreciate it, Ron, if you'd check with me before you do anything in the VC department. I make out the orders here. All you have to do is see we get the deliveries."

"I was only trying to help, Jim," Ron answered, "to take some of the paperwork off your back. I thought it would speed up things if the order forms were already made out when you received the stuff. I thought I was helping you by learning how to make out the forms when the stuff came in."

"Well, I'd rather do that myself, Ron. After all, I'm responsible for this area."

"Sorry."

This kind of response often occurs in jobs where the work cannot fill the whole day or in jobs where the worker feels threatened if his routine is in any way violated. It also occurs from time to time in ill-defined jobs or in situations where two workers are given the same kind of assignment in competition. Most bureaucracies build up this kind of protective attitude toward the assignments: "Ethel takes care of the orders. See Jack if you want to discuss inventory."

Many jobs also carry with them certain aspects of authority and any encroachment on that authority will be deeply resented.

70

Nevertheless, if you intend to move on in the organization, you would do well to find out what is involved in other jobs— what skills and experience are called for and what kind of backgrounds and aptitudes those who hold these jobs have. While many will not allow you to "help" them with their jobs, they will usually be glad to tell you how hard they work and what they do.

Knowing what associates and superiors do, understanding what skills and experience must be developed to hold those jobs, gives you a chance to assess your own work better, its value and how it fits into the scheme of things. Even if the territorial imperative will not allow you to try some of the work of your associates, you can learn a great deal from watching how they handle their jobs, from showing an interest and from asking questions.

As you will see when we move to Part III, all jobs include relationship problems as well as work problems, and when you try to widen your work horizons in the initial jobs you have, use your tact and knowledge of your associates to learn all you can in such a way that they do not feel threatened by your efforts.

Techniques and tactics to keep you alert to opportunities in other jobs around you

1. No matter what your job is, look at the other jobs around you.

2. Do not allow the group or individuals to confine you to "minding your own business." Your business is the enterprise as a whole, which includes their jobs and anyone else's. You do not have to be chairman of the board to take an interest in other jobs.

3. Be helpful if you can without offending or threatening associates and be tactful and understanding of their territorial imperatives.

71

4. At the very least take an interest in what they are doing and try to imagine yourself in their shoes and understand what skills and experience are needed and what you would do, if you had their jobs.

Going Up

It is important that you grow in your job. It is important that you know what possibilities there are in the organization where you work. It is important that you know who can help you move on and how this is done.

You must know the career path in your organization. In a manufacturing company the levels may be foreman, superintendent, manager, assistant vice-president, vice-president and on to the top. In a bank the grades may run from cashier to assistant in operations, loan officers or the equivalent in other departments to assistant vice-president, vice-president, senior vice-president, executive vice-president and on to the top. In a talent organization such as a broadcasting network or advertising agency the career path may not be so structured and your rise may depend more on a special talent or on a project that brings in clients or brings you to the attention of the top people. In a professional firm the career path may move through four or five stages from staff through supervisor or manager or director to partner. And in the partnership there are also grades.

But knowing the titles in a career path is not enough. You must learn why certain persons succeed so well in that organization, what they did that singled them out, what they are known for. If wrongly exploited, of course, ambition can be ugly and dehumanizing. But it can also be a beautiful thing, and it has brought every outstanding person to his or her place in the sun. Without it there is little improvement, little progress. With it the movers and shakers of the world and the great creators have given us the best our world has to offer. In our work world, ambition is called motivation, because ambition is a powerful and somewhat frightening word, but lacking motivation, you are dead.

One of our personnel directors told us this story.

He had an assistant from Puerto Rico who was superb at her job, but he noticed she seemed to be under stress and very unhappy. So one day he called her into his office.

"Carmelita, what is the matter?"
"Nothing," she answered.

He allowed her to sit there a minute.

"Maybe talking about it will help?" he said.
"Mr. Quiller, I've been here two years. I've done my job as best I can. I make no trouble. I keep to myself, don' bother anybody, dress right, good manners, but nobody come to me an' say, 'Carmelita, you good, I give you more money and promote you.' Nobody . . ."

So he sat back and looked at her.

"Carmelita," he said, "I am going to disillusion you a bit. I am going to give you the facts of life. You've done a fine job with me and I'm very happy with you. I don't want to lose you. I've given you one raise and maybe can give you one or two more in this job but that's as far as I can go. I have no job here that I can promote you to. So why would I want to lose you? So if I hadn't called you in because I like and respect you, nobody, not even I would have come to you and said, 'Carmelita, you're a valuable employee. Here's more money and a promotion.' Here there are a lot of people good in their work who want to get on, but the organization, even if satisfied with them, is not going to hand out their rewards on a silver platter. You're going to have to go out and get them, maybe even fight for them.

"You've been sitting here quietly, doing your work and waiting. You know nobody here except me and two others in this office. Now you have to get out and get to know this company. You have to learn what there is out there and what you want. You have to see who the opinion and taste leaders are in this world and learn what you can from them. You have to see who are your competitors and what they are doing to get on. You have to show you can survive and be happy in this place, Carmelita. If you were a bright ambitious young man, I wouldn't have to tell you all this, but it makes no difference that you're a well brought up, pretty young woman. We are an equal opportunity employer, but it's the opportunity that is equal, not the rewards and promotions.

"I will help you—though I don't want to lose you—when you have gone out and learned about the company and our business, when you have learned where you want to go and what you want to do and who you really are in this work world. But until then—and you'll have to get going, get to know others on your lunch hour, take courses at night, and so on—until then, stay here and be happy."

Carmelita's is an exaggerated case, though representative, of the way we are brought up. We are brought up to believe that if we just do a good job, the organization or community or the world will come to us and say, "You've done a good job. Here's your reward." That, our advisers say, is not quite the way it is. Going up depends on a lot of things besides doing good work and behaving well. Just as important, and often more so, are the relationships we are able to develop.

Let us now turn to Part III, "Relationships—Thirty Things

You Should Know about an Organization and Its People.''
Your career path should point upward. These are some of the
things you should know, if you want to go up.

SELF-ASSESSMENT ON PART II, "THE WORK"

The experiences, principles, tactics and techniques that were discussed in this section become operative only when you can apply
them to your own work situation. This self-assessment gives you a
chance to relate them to your own work and career. Apply them to
your job. Relevant discussions are indicated in the suggested answers and references to these self-assessments on pages 267–270.

1. What specific measures will give you a basis for judging
   your competence in your present job?
2. Can you list two of your functional skills and five of your
   management skills?
3. List the two time-wasting habits that most interfere with
   your work.
4. What is the measure of efficiency in your job?
5. What is the measure of effectiveness in your job?
6. How often do you need to take time off for family reasons?
7. How often do you bring your work home?
8. How many vacations or holidays have you missed because of your work?
9. How often do you have periods of inability to function,
   periods of goofing off?
10. What work characteristics have you been able to adopt

of the person you consider the most productive worker in your group?

11. What aspects of your job have you been able to quantify—in such terms as tasks completed per day, calls made per week, reports turned in per month or the like?

12. What measures have you taken during your periods of anxiety to meet this kind of stress?

13. What parts of your job do you like best?

14. What parts of your job do you dislike most?

15. How often do you feel bored on the job and what measures do you take to counteract this feeling?

16. You are called in to your boss's office and asked to sit down. "John," your boss says, "Bob Metzell in St. Louis has asked me to let you consider a job with his division there. He considers you just the right man for their new marketing area, and I've told him I'd put the proposition to you. Now you don't have to go. Your work here is fine and I'd like to keep you." What questions should you ask and what should be your response to the offer?

17. You go in to see your boss. You have been in manufacturing now for three years and you feel you would like to move to marketing to broaden your skills and your background. You say, "Ron, I like the work here but I think I've become a bit specialized and I'd like to learn more about how we market our products. Would it be possible to be transferred into marketing?" Your boss sits back and looks at you quizzically. "Don't like it here, huh, John? Want to go out with the glamour boys, is that it?" Did you make a mistake in going in with this request?

18. "Listen, Jack," Harry Bright says cheerfully, "I know I haven't paid too much attention to you lately. Your

work is very good, but we've all been busy. Maybe it is time for you to get a promotion, but I can't help you right now. Everything is at sixes and sevens. I just don't have the time, but keep up the good work, keep your nose clean and we'll get around to you yet. Be patient.'' What should you do?

PART III

□

RELATIONSHIPS
—Thirty Things You Should Know about an Organization and Its People

Of the four areas of things you should know about to hold and protect a job: the work, relationships, the outside world and legal remedies, the most important and most complex in the opinion of our advisers, is the area of relationships.

Whether you survive in the work world of our society will depend a great deal on your being able to relate to others.

You may be a fine worker, skillful in your job, your intentions may be the best, your integrity and character first rate, but if you do not know how to get along with others, how to understand and relate to the organization, its beliefs, traditions, ways of doing things, its morals, its manners, the things it will tolerate and the things it will not, its policies and most of all the kind of people it cherishes and requires, you will not last long. In any organization, to do the job right, you must become a respected part of the organization itself. This is a hard truth for some of us to swallow. Many of us have dismissed this part of the job as simply politics or conniving or organizational nonsense. It is not. In an organization, no job is done alone. All of us depend on others to do any job given us.

Your organization depends on your ability to relate to others so that the work of the whole may be completed. The higher you go in an organization, the more important your work, the more important will be your ability to establish and maintain fruitful relationships. Power lies in what is granted you by others. Influence lies wholly in what others will grant you. Authority may be given you by a position: it can rarely be exercised until you have a good working relationship with others. This is an area that is more subtle, more complex and generally more important than any other area of your working life.

We therefore have dealt with it in more detail and with more variety than with the other areas. We present here the things you should know about an organization and its people.

The World According to the Boss

In work-world relationships, your boss is usually the major factor in your work life and may cause you the most problems and sometimes the greatest anxiety.

It is not that he or she means to be a burden to you. It is simply the nature of the relationship. In any career with its series of jobs, you will have several different bosses, some good, some not so good, some supportive or even protective, one or two perhaps, if you are unlucky, hostile or even destructive. A boss may even become a mentor, giving you a wider view of the world, and when that person goes up, he or she may take you along.

It is, however, important that you understand the boss's world, values and problems. Your boss reports to someone just as you do; even a boss who is chairman or chief executive officer in effect reports to the board of directors and ultimately to the shareholders and the public. We are a gregarious species, we humans, and we live in a hierarchical world, and none of us, if we wish to live fully, walks alone. Many of us dream of being "independent," of being our own boss, but even entrepreneurs have bosses, the most difficult, unpredictable and quixotic of all, the marketplace. And they study their bosses and try to understand them as assiduously as any ambitious middle manager.

You—whatever your job—report to someone and you should learn what that someone's world is, what that person feels about the world and even what the boss's job is, because you may want sometime to succeed him or her in it. You must also learn what your boss believes your job is.

One of our advisers who is a personnel director told us the following story:

> A young woman employed in the company as an administrative assistant came to him. Her record was excellent, but she was shaking with anger. He got her seated and calmed down. "All right," he said, "what is it?"
>
> "I'm overworked and underpaid," she burst out. "So I finally had it. I went in to Mr. Wilmer and I told him off. I told him what I would not do on this job. I'd do all the things that the job specifications demand, as described in the manual, but I would no longer spend hours over his budget, stay late to rework this and that when that's what someone else should be doing. . . ." And she continued down the rather formidable list. "So," she concluded, "I told him what I would do and what I wouldn't do."
>
> "What did he say?" the personnel director asked.
>
> "He didn't say anything. He was too stunned," she answered.
>
> "Catherine," the personnel director said after a silence, "I believe you have just cut your own throat. Let me ask you something. Do you know the man Mr. Wilmer reports to, Mr. Conrad?"
>
> "No," she answered.
>
> "Well, Mr. Conrad is a brilliant, hard-driving vice-president. He heads a difficult, thriving part of the business. Now supposing Mr. Wilmer went into his boss, Mr. Conrad, and told him what you've just told your boss, what he will do and what he won't do? Just

83

how long do you think Mr. Wilmer would have a job?''

Catherine was silent a moment.

"I never thought of it that way," she said after a pause. "But it isn't fair."

"As someone said, Catherine, life isn't fair," the personnel director replied. "But that's the way it is. Now you march right back in to see Mr. Wilmer before he hangs himself and tell him you'll do any job he gives you. Unless what you are being asked is illicit or illegal, the manager decides what your job is, Catherine—that's part of his job. You'll decide what the jobs of those who report to you are—they will not tell you what their jobs are. You are not a cleaning woman saying, 'I don't do windows.' Mr. Wilmer probably likes you, Catherine, so he will understand your outburst. Possibly he has felt that way toward the work Mr. Conrad forces on him from time to time. But wait until you're chairman of the board before you tell Mr. Wilmer what that job is supposed to be.''

Look at your boss's world, our advisers tell us. You will understand your own job better and you will become more effective in the organization.

Factors to consider in dealing successfully with your boss

1. Your boss reports to someone. It will help to know who this someone is, what the person is like and what pressures and demands are put on your boss.

2. Your boss's job involves certain responsibilities. They may be responsibilities unrelated to your own duties. If you know what they are, you will understand why your boss does certain things and how you yourself may play a larger role in the total job.

3. Your boss, whether you realize it or not, is dependent on

you in certain respects. It is important that you understand exactly in what ways he or she is dependent on you and your work.

4.   If you can make your boss look good, you may make a powerful friend in the organization.

The World According to the Company

Every organization is a culture unto itself. It is a community you enter with its own beliefs, policies, dreams, objectives, myths and ways of doing things.

Years ago in one large organization headquarters, the photographs of the chairman and the president adorned the walls of every office with two windows or more. This type of hierarchical chauvinism is no longer practiced, but that does not mean that in even the most seemingly informal and democratic organization there are not rules, customs, myths and understandings that you violate at your peril. If it is the custom in a swinging organization on the West Coast to appear at the office in slacks and a sport shirt and you show up in a three-piece suit with tie and white button-down shirt, they may applaud your originality but they will not feel you are one of them.

Not long ago at a famous professional firm, it was required in the metropolitan offices that we wear a hat when going to a client's office. Those days are long gone and some of us do not even own a hat anymore. In some offices it was decreed that women not wear what the older partners called "men's pants" at the office. Those days also are gone together with the older partners, but in every organization there are sometimes decreed, sometimes hidden and difficult-to-perceive customs and rules not only in the way you dress but also in the kind of language you use, your manners, your way of looking at things, even your way of thinking. It is not that they are trying to brainwash you. It is simply that this is, in a phrase, "the custom of the country.'' If you cannot eventually adapt and be happy in these customs, beliefs, rules, myths and dreams, you will in all probability not be able to get anything done or to succeed in that organization.

"Jim Tanner and I started together in this company," John Breen, an executive vice-president in a very successful consumer products company told us. "Jim was a good friend of mine in the old days, intelligent, slow moving and easygoing, but . . . well, this was not the company for him, and I told him so a long time ago. But he held on. He didn't want to move, and he's been passed over, while I've gone up. I see him now and again, but we're not friends anymore. He looks at me with something like hatred. He's become bitter. He feels we're all out to get him, or that he has enemies who have been holding him back. That's not so. He is simply not of the temperament, not really fast enough on his feet, for this kind of business. He's good at what he does, but he moves too slowly. He should have left the company the first time I was pushed up and he was left behind. He taught me a lot of what I know, but I'm the kind they want. They pick drivers like me and Hack Benson, Jim's new boss. That's the way they are. Maybe it makes the company a less admirable place, more crassly commercial than it should be, and maybe Jim's right to hate and look down on this completely marketing-oriented type of company. But that's the way the company is. Those are the facts of life, and nobody's going to change this organization's way—it's been very successful. Jim never understood this company and he should never have stayed. Now maybe it's too late . . .''

People who remain in the wrong company often feel that it

was office politics that did them in. They do good work but somehow they seem to be passed over, they never quite catch the brass ring. This is not office politics; it is simply a mismatching of the person's persona and the organization's ambience. Jim Tanner should have gone to a place where his slow, easygoing personality could flower and where he could do the company the most good.

"Well, I'll tell you," the professor said, removing his pipe and looking thoughtful. "I suppose Harry Croft was a good teacher, and we needed someone with his background in the business world, but he rubbed a lot of us the wrong way. First of all, he didn't have the credentials for this kind of university, and he was loud and brash, and his remarks about old Professor Harrington, who used to be head of this department, were completely uncalled for. This is a university, not a merchandising outfit, and a love of research is not considered a crime. Furthermore, he could not speak our language. He did not even understand that he had grossly insulted his own department head with his references to ivory-tower dummies who have never been in the real world. And he could never understand the understated way we express ourselves. To him, the comment 'That was not really in the best interests of the university' seemed a rather mild remark. In our world, that is the strongest condemnation we can express. I don't know. It was too bad. But maybe you can see now why Harry's contract was not renewed."

Every organization—in business, in education, in politics— has its own tempo and ambience, its own culture and way of life. Be sure you understand the culture and way of life of your company.

A primer on ways to tell whether you are in the right organization

1. Do you share the same values? This, of course, does not mean that you approve of or believe in everything the organization does, but it does mean: Do you in general admire and believe in its basic policies and its economic legitimacy? On the other hand, if you are a flaming liberal in a basically conservative company or the company's policies seem utterly wrong to you or your associates strike you as asinine or nincompoops or fools or worse, then you are probably in the wrong company.

2. Regardless of how good the company seems to you or how well you may like your associates, do you find organization life stifling? Do you feel smothered or panicky trying to keep the nine to five hours and the company rituals? If so, you may not be suited to the ordinary life of business organizations. You may be better suited to the riskier entrepreneurial life or to the less structured academic world or to the professional life dealing with clients.

3. Are you born to pursue one of the arts—to become an actor, a musician, a dancer, a film director, a sculptor? It is not simply unusual talent that is necessary here but the compulsive personality that will make your life unfulfilled if you cannot pursue your art, that will make you pursue that art under any and all circumstances. Since your art comes first, you may have to support it in jobs that leave you free to pursue it and you may find yourself unable to pursue a career in a business organization that cannot accommodate such a pursuit.

It is important to know yourself well enough and to understand the culture of the company you have become a part of in order to survive and succeed in that career or in any career you have formulated for yourself.

88

Office Politics

"In that place," Art Morris said, "you have to sit facing the door or someone will stab you in the back. The conniving, the plotting, the putting you down behind your back you wouldn't believe."

"What happened?" the executive recruiter said.

"Well, as you may have heard, a new man was brought in as president," Art Morris replied. "I suppose the board felt we needed shaking up. This new guy was a gung-ho, nonlistener—a driver—and he started all of us competing with each other. But he was not very perceptive. He liked to see people jumping. Now unfortunately, some of our best people aren't jumpers. They like to work and produce but they don't necessarily like to look as of they were the hottest pistols in town. And they aren't good at playing games. I got tired of playing games too. I'm a pretty premium product in this field, and I won in the competition with the politician they had me up against, but here I am looking for something else. The place is a jungle."

"Give me an example?"

"Well, my buddy, as Barry Sullivan called himself, apparently got to our new president early," Art Morris said. "And it seems that I am supposed to have been responsible for the Mark 802 Project, which our new president rightly considers a disaster. Oh, Barry didn't actually come right out and say I initiated it. Apparently he hinted, however, that at one time it had been my baby. As it turns out, one of the managers on that project, which is now being phased out, has raised hell about the way he was treated and in a pretty hairy memo outlining the circumstances of the project named Barry as the man who had supported and misrepresented to him the whole project. It seems I was

89

exonerated; the president has lost confidence in Barry and I am in his good graces again. But I'm ready to look around. That's only one of the musical chairs that's being played at national headquarters. The politics there are getting ferocious . . ."

Politics means people, and there is no organization that does not involve some form of political maneuvering. Where people have a vested interest, where they are under pressure, where they are eager to advance and their livelihood is at stake, there will be those who use unfair or dishonest or devious methods to advance or protect themselves. Good organizations have a minimum of such dishonest or devious maneuvering, and the best people usually rise. Bad organizations, which do not define the work properly or put people under pressure or make unreasonable demands, and organizations in the midst of change and turmoil nurture such devious and throat cutting political maneuvering. They tend to lose their best men and women and to promote those who simply know how to please and to play to the prejudices and stupidities of their superiors.

If you know your organization and its people, if you are "one of us," if you yourself have made friends and understand the motives and objectives of those in the organization, you are not likely to become a victim of political machination, particularly if you have learned how to communicate in that organization.

There are, of course, situations where you may lose out because of the luck of the draw—your skills or your work is not what is needed at that time or under those circumstances or someone with exceptional talent or experience is brought in over you to do something you and others are not equipped to do; that is not office politics. If you are willing to lie low when your skills are not needed and to accept gracefully such traumatic situations, you will usually survive and eventually go forward when the organization must turn once more to you.

90

**A few basic principles for understanding and protecting
yourself in office politics**

Remember this about office politics:

1. There is no organization without politics. Politics means
people, and people have different goals, different desires
and different stresses. To understand the politics in your
organization, you must understand the people around
you—their ambitions, their temperaments, their needs,
their desires, their goals. Make it your business to understand your associates. Go to lunch with them. Stay in the
flow of gossip and rumor. Learn to be one of the gang.

2. Be aware of the company's values. Those who transgress
the company values find the political atmosphere unten-
able. They find themselves passed over in promotions and
in many ways subtly penalized and in the end rejected as
not being "one of us." Many persons who were done in
by transgressing company values feel that it was "office
politics" that destroyed their career in that organization.
Consider the company's values and customs. Learn to
live with them, if you can.

3. It is possible that you may be caught in a political situation that you are not fully aware of and that puts you in a
no-win situation—a power struggle in which you find
yourself on the wrong side, a question of loyalty that
cannot be resolved in your favor, the machinations of a
malevolent associate who for reasons of ambition or dislike sets out to destroy your career. We outline some of
these situations in the following sections: "Why Doesn't
He/She Like Me?" "The Killer Boss," "Being Frank,"
"Being Devious," "He's Out to Get Me," "Troublemaker" and others. In 90 percent of the cases of malicious political maneuvers, you will survive and the politician will be seen for what he is, but the sections indicated
suggest certain steps you can take.

Communicating

"If there is one other thing I wish I had learned at the Harvard Business School," a top executive told us, "it is how to communicate. I learned a lot of the most useful things I know about the work world and organizations there, but I didn't learn how to communicate, and it may be that this is something you have to learn by experience, you have to learn it in life—maybe it can't be taught . . ."

This executive is expressing something that almost every thoughtful person in the work world experiences at one time or another—the puzzling difficulty of communicating. Over and over again you hear, "You've got to learn how to communicate to get on in this organization." Or, "He's good in the job but he doesn't know how to communicate." The fact is you cannot get on or rise in an organization unless you learn how to communicate.

This, of course, is true, but few of us and few of those who teach us seem to know what communicating means. Most of our waking life, of course, is spent communicating, that is, trying to reach others. Courses in communicating usually stress improvement in speaking and writing, but there are excellent speakers and fine writers who cannot communicate. They do not know who to reach or how to reach them and they may not have a message that will be of value or interest to those they are trying to reach.

In an organization, communicating means establishing good relationships and reaching the right persons with the right messages at the right time, usually to get something done. To do this you must know the organization and its people; you must know who the taste and opinion leaders are in that organization; you must know how to become "one of us"; and you must know what should be communicated and at what level.

The following passage from a book* on communicating expresses this truth:

* *Communicating at the Top*—John Wiley & Sons, N.Y., 1979.

Among the most baffling questions facing those who must reach others are: In what form and through what means can the individual or the group be reached? What channel or what medium does one use to get the message through? Experience seems to show it is not enough to have eloquence or skill in language; one must also know how to put these skills into the most effective channels. One must understand the levels and forms of communicating in the business, social, and organizational worlds and how to employ them.

It is often a source of wonder that certain men who do not express themselves well and are not eloquent can so frequently put over their messages so effectively in an organization. The answer generally lies in their knowledge of the forms and channels and of their use in that organization. The beautifully worded message sent in the form of a memorandum at a certain level of organization may have precisely the opposite effect intended or no effect at all because that message should have been transmitted only at the informal level and probably by word of mouth. A great idea may lie floating in the Sargasso Sea of informal communication, when it should have had a full-scale presentation before a board of directors. A substantial treatment which belongs in a book in the great world may be dissipated in a dozen little manuals or instruction guides because no one understood the potentialities of the main form.

Here the effectiveness of language, no matter how eloquent, and of substance, no matter how valuable, is destroyed by not understanding or suiting the proper form and medium to the content and not being aware of the proper channels through which people reach each other.

In all organizations in the work world, there are three levels and seven basic forms (with variations) by which people reach each other.

The three levels are: first, the mysterious world of unorganized communicating through which some 70 percent of all communicating in an organization takes place, that is, the world of the grapevine, of rumor, of phatic communicating, the communicating used to establish relationships; second, the world of formal communicating established by the organization using one or another or all of the seven forms; and third, the level at which opinion and taste leaders can be reached, where art and style are important.

The first level, the world of unorganized communicating, is by far the most important level. It is here that you establish relationships, plug into the rumor mills and the grapevine, make friends and even get most of the work of the organization done. Consider these examples taken from the above study:

> "Bill, how about scrounging up some extra parts for Number 4 shop for tomorrow. I know it's not according to the book, but we'll do your group a favor when the Benson order comes in." Result: a shop meets its quota on time.

> "Well, I'll tell you, Jim, he was with me for a while, but I just . . . well I don't know. I wouldn't want to queer his chances." Result: the man about whom they are speaking does not get the promotion.

At the second level, the level of organized, recognized forms in that organization, seven forms are generally used, each sometimes specified, sometimes developed according to custom. These forms are quite simply: *short message forms*—letter and telecommunications; *conferences*—informal or formal meetings; *memorandums and reports; policy or instruction manuals; speeches or talks* before others in or out of the organization; *articles* for publication; and finally *books* for the communicating and preserving of material valuable in your organization or profession.

In each organization most of these forms have been tailored to the specifications or customs of the organization. Thus, if

94

you are sending a report to an organization, it should be in the form in which the organization's people are accustomed to receive their reports. When people are used to seeing something in a certain form, they tend to accept it more readily and find it easier to get the content.

The third level of communicating is not given to all of us, since it requires both art and style. This is the level at which most of the world's taste and opinion leaders can be reached. Opinion leaders are sensitive to the original, the unusual, and to high quality. All people develop their own art and style as best they can. Personality has a great deal to do with it as does exceptional talent and even genius. Distinguished writing or communicating is the product of distinguished minds and is not given to us all, even the most hardworking and deserving. But good writing has certain characteristics in the actual use of language that, in the words of the study mentioned above, may be described and illustrated as follows:

> It is usually simple and basic. It usually drives to the heart of important meanings. It has color, candor, and sweep.
>
> George Orwell, the noted British author, in a review, converted a famous passage of the Bible into the kind of ordinary decent business jargon which we use. Here it is, as Orwell rendered it:
>
> Objective consideration of contemporary phenomena compels the conclusion that success or failure in competitive activities exhibits no tendency to be commensurate with innate capacity, but that a considerable element of the unpredictable must inevitably be taken into account.

There is nothing especially wrong with this. A little heavy perhaps. It speaks to us in the generalities we so dearly love. It uses our rather ponderous wording. It lacks color. But here is how Ecclesiastes said it—the difference between ordinary writing and great writing:

> I returned and saw under the sun that the race is not to the swift nor the battle to the strong, neither yet bread to the wise nor yet

95

riches to men of understanding nor yet favor to men of skill but time and chance happeneth to them all.

It is at this level—at this third level—that the whole person is reached.

Techniques, tactics and strategies in communicating

1. Learn how to operate at the first level of communicating, the level of unorganized, general, person-to-person communicating, which is the most important type of communication in any organization (see "The Grapevine").

2. Learn to prepare and use at least some of the seven basic forms of communicating employed at the formal organized level.

3. If your gifts are sufficient to operate at the third level, you will reach opinion leaders and you can sway the world (see "Opinion Leaders").

Supervisory Styles

Perhaps no insight has been more useful to understanding relationships and our own approach to others than the simplified "modes" described by Dr. Eric Berne in his famed book *Games People Play*. Dr. Berne's modes are based on the insights of Freud on our psychic makeup. As is well known, Freud divided our psyche into the id, the raw, animal child in us; the ego, the self-identity, the adult part of our nature; and the superego, the authority, the censor aspect of our nature. Dr. Berne brought us the simpler, very useful insight that the first, the id, is the child in us; the second the ego is the adult in us, facing a world of equals, and the third mode is the parent in us, the authority figure to others.

All of us embody these three modes when interacting with others. We may become children with certain parental or authority figures in our lives or in certain situations. We usually interact as adults in the ordinary routines of our lives, and sometimes we become parents or authority figures to others.

In the organization world these three modes give us some insight into the way we behave toward others and the way others behave toward us in a hierarchical world.

"What's he complaining about now?" the executive secretary asks.

"The world's gone to hell in a handbasket," Vivian Wheeler, Mr. Wilmot's secretary, replies. "The reports didn't come in. Burt Chandler's acting up again. He wishes they'd do something about this, they'd do something about that . . ."

"The man's a professional crybaby," the executive secretary sighs. "I don't know how you put up with it."

"Oh, he's all right at heart," Vivian Wheeler answers. "He's just a big baby."

"Well, he's a holy terror too most of the time."

Here is a boss who interacts in the child mode with his secretary and in the parental or authoritative mode with those who report to him.

That this man's wife will eventually leave him, since she has children and does not need an extra child of forty-six in the family, and that Wilmot will eventually marry Vivian Wheeler, since she likes to interact with him as mama, is beyond the scope of our study, but it illustrates the importance of understanding how someone is approaching you— whether as child, adult or parent figure. Let us look at one more example of a supervisor who interacted with his people as a child. This passage is taken from *Corporate Lives*. The speaker is the chief executive of a major corporation who remembers one of his bosses and how he learned to handle him:

I was sent out as a production engineer to a plant in a bleak area where there was little to do but work long hours during those Depression years. One of the first bosses I had at the plant was a big burly Irishman with a very short fuse. He was known and feared, and when I was assigned to him, I knew I'd have to learn to live with this character. He had the habit of blowing up on the slightest provocation. He would go out on the line and he'd invariably see something amiss, or an order delayed, or something not just as he thought it should be, then he would, without finding out why or listening to any reason, immediately call in his chief assistant—me—and start yelling about it. It would do no good to try to tell him the reason, even if it were a very simple reason or a very good sensible reason. He would shout right through the attempted explanation.

Fortunately, I developed a method of coping with this man and he grew to like me and trust me. My method was very simple. When he would call me in and start on his tirade, I would sit down and pull out a notebook and pencil and I would take down what he was saying or take notes about the difficulty. I wouldn't say anything. I'd just listen, and pretty soon he would have blown off the steam and he'd settle down. Then I'd say: "I'll go out and find out what happened, and I'll come back and report to you."

Then I'd see what it was, have it fixed up or get the explanation. Later, I'd tell him, and he'd usually have forgotten about it or he'd say: "Well, that's all right," or "As long as it's fixed up," or "Forget it–it wasn't important." The thing was he needed someone to listen to him when he got excited. Pressures got to him easily and he blew up when anything seemed to him to be going wrong. I learned a valuable lesson from him. I learned how important it was to understand the person as well as what he's saying. My pulling out my pad and taking notes and listening to him were what calmed him down. If I'd tried to argue with him or point out to him any unreasonableness in his response, I'd

98

have gotten nowhere—except perhaps the gate. So I learned to live with him and he took a liking to me. Later he was transferred. With his temperament he had gotten as far as he was going, but he recommended me for his job as he moved on.

These examples may illustrate how important it is to understand how someone is approaching you—whether as a child, an adult or a parent figure—and this will serve as an introduction to a few other things you should know about relationships in an organization, namely what forms of supervisory styles seem to obtain there.

Ever since Douglas McGregor put forth his popular x-y grid analyzing supervisory types, the x being the authoritarian or dictator type of boss, the y being the participative, supportive sort of boss who sets a climate in which everyone can actualize himself through his work, methods of supervision have been analyzed and reanalyzed in great profusion and detail. You will gain by knowing what type of atmosphere, what form of supervision, you find yourself most comfortable with and by knowing, even if only in a general way, the style of supervision favored in the organization you work for. Of course, there will be good or bad supervisors to be found, and they will be using all styles of supervision, the quality of which depends more on the quality of the person than on the style of supervision.

In the mid-seventies, Michael Maccoby, the social psychologist, published his findings of a study he made of organization types in the business world in a book entitled *The Gamesman*. He found four psychological types in modern corporations: the *craftsman,* the *jungle fighter,* the *company man* and the *gamesman.* The craftsman he described as holding the traditional values: the work ethic, respect for people, concern for quality and thrift, and his interest is in the process, the making of something. He is a maker. That is his orientation.

The jungle fighter's goal is power. He experiences the work world as a jungle where he must fight to survive. He views his associates as accomplices or enemies. Maccoby found two types of jungle fighters: the lions and the foxes. The lions build empires; the foxes next in the corporate hierarchy move ahead by stealth and politicking.

The company man Maccoby recognized in the old organization man we all know whose sense of identity is based on being part of the organization. Added to "For God, for Country and for Yale" is the company man's "For Exxon, IBM or Price Waterhouse."

Maccoby defined the gamesman as the new man, whose main interest is the challenge, competitive activity in which he can prove himself. He likes to take risks and to push others. He responds to work and life as a game. It was Maccoby's conclusion that organizations need all types except the jungle fighter; they need craftsmen and company men and women but mostly they need gamesmen, a sort of entrepreneurial character in his approach to the game of business.

This is an extreme simplification of Maccoby's study of the psychological types found in organizations of the work world, but his study and dozens of others on supervisory styles may be useful and enlightening to the jobholder who wishes a career in an organization.

Techniques and strategies in dealing with your superior

1. Study the supervisory atmosphere in your organization. Is it generally participative? Is it generally authoritarian? Follow that style to get things done.

2. Determine the management style of your own boss and his or her supervisors. This will enable you to respond sensibly to the boss's efforts to get things done.

3. Shape your responses to the style of management. There are good managers and bad managers in each style. It is

difficult to work under a bad manager, regardless of the style of management. Nevertheless, you can handle almost any management style, if you understand it, and you yourself can learn to manage your relations with your boss in the same way you can manage all your other relationships in the organization (see "Managing Up").

Listening

"I tell you, Jeff," Ron Bellamy is saying, "this has been tried before. That Martelle Program was tried back in the seventies. I could give you the names of ten or so engineers who had experience with it, and not one of them will tell you it has any chance of working under the circumstances we have here."

"But don't you think . . ."

"And furthermore, I believe we went all over that in a meeting last fall when Crandall was with us, and it just seems to me that we shouldn't go all through that again."

"But, Bev . . ."

"She thinks if she's just persistent enough, I'll see it her way. And I just wish someone would pay attention to what I tell them in these matters."

"But, Ron, that . . ."

"And furthermore, just the other day I had occasion to talk . . ."

"But, Ron . . ."

"You may think I'm being arbitrary about this, but someone has to put his foot down sometime . . ."

[Shouts] "Ron!"

"What is it, Jeff?"

"That's not what I came in to ask you."

Listening. Listening is half of communicating and sometimes the more important half. Studies have shown that some

101

70 to 80 percent of our waking lives is spent communicating, about half of that, 45 percent, is listening, as against 30 percent of communicating in speaking, 16 percent in reading and 9 percent in writing. To the jobholder, listening has become one of the most important tools he will need, not only in work but also in relationships with those in the organization. Dr. Lyman K. Steil of the University of Minnesota, who developed and presents the listening seminars for the Sperry Corporation, a program that has formed the basis of their famous "listening" ads, has pointed out that, by any given test, people do not know how to listen. A number of studies and tests of the listening abilities of thousands of students and hundreds of business and professional people indicate that immediately after listening to someone talk, the average person will have heard only part of what was said and correctly understood only part of what was heard no matter how carefully he thought he was listening. Testing showed that the average person will listen effectively at only about a 25 percent level over a period of time.

Dr. Steil, in his book *Listening—It Can Change Your Life,* has described the basic building blocks of listening: *sensing,* the actual hearing of the voice; *interpreting,* the understanding of what was said; *evaluating,* the assessing of the importance or import of the message; and *responding,* letting the sender know that the message has been received. He estimates that in our modern result-oriented society, most of us fail at almost all these levels. We screen out or do not hear some of what is said; we do not interpret correctly what was meant; we often do not evaluate properly, dismissing things that might be important to us, and many of us respond but do so inappropriately since we have only half-heard, have misinterpreted and have not evaluated properly what someone is trying to tell us.

In any job listening is of major importance. In a career it is crucial. As you go up in your career, listening to others becomes more and more essential to your job. The executive must be a sensitive listener, not only for his own sake but because his position of authority affects other people's lives and careers. There are too many Ron Bellamys in the working world, people who listen only to their own voices. Learn to listen early and protect that valuable tool. You will become a popular and sought after jobholder.

Techniques, tactics and strategies that will make you a better listener

1. *Establish an agreeable atmosphere.* This means put the speaker at ease and hold the talk where the person you are listening to can feel relaxed.

2. *Be prepared to hear the other person through on his own terms.* Many of the messages most worth listening to are not always presented well or in an agreeable tone of voice. The good listener is tolerant of the speaker's difficulties.

3. *Be prepared on the subject to be discussed.* It is surprising how many of us fail to take the time to look into the background in even the sketchiest way of a subject that is to be brought to our attention.

4. *Evaluate the speaker and make allowances for his circumstances.* Most of us make a quick evaluation of any speaker to assess how much of what he will say can be expected to be either relevant or valuable to us. But the good listener is tolerant of any other circumstances—the wrong tie, notes forgotten, severe strain. Good listeners make allowances and then listen.

5. *Avoid getting mentally sidetracked when subjects are not central to the issue or touch on sore points.* A good listener takes the valuable points and holds in abeyance those aspects which are irrelevant or arouse emotion. He is able to listen to those aspects of a subject about which

103

he does not agree. A poor listener tunes out anything that he does not agree with or that arouses him emotionally.

6. *Listen for and summarize basic ideas.* No device is better for grasping what is being said than that of summarizing mentally the main points. Make this a habit.

7. *Restate the substance of what you have heard to the speaker.* This technique for clarifying and pinning down the substance of what is said is perhaps the most effective of the techniques for the listener. It has prevented misunderstanding and fastens the real import of the message.

8. *Takes notes, where possible.* The shortest pencil outlasts the longest memory.

Being Frank

In the work world, whenever you hear the word *frankly,* you can almost count on its being followed by bad news.

"Frankly, I never thought the project would fly," Doug Casper is saying. "Frankly, we took a beating on that."

"Frankly," Hal Webster begins, "I have to tell you, Harry, your work has not been up to par lately . . ."

"Frankly," Kit Johnson says, "I must say exactly what I mean. We don't think you're very good at this."

Being frank, saying exactly what you mean, has been given, it seems to us, a somewhat undeserved reputation. The speaker seems to imply a moral superiority, and except for the object of his frankness, those listening seem to applaud him. "He speaks right out. He doesn't mince words," is usually said with admiration or relish. But in the work world, as in life, the stresses are great enough, the problems of getting through the day heavy enough, that being frank and speaking right out are probably an unnecessary burden to the recipient and usually counterproductive.

Being frank may relieve your own feelings, but the question

to ask oneself on a job is: What good will it do for you to be frank, to give them a piece of your mind?

If the answer is none, then pause.

The next question to ask is: What harm will it do?

If the answer is considerable or even some, then forget it.

Business and the work world have their euphemisms and ceremonies, which seem to many stupid and insincere. We do not demote someone for incompetence; we say, "His special qualifications make him invaluable in a new assignment." We do not fire people, we allow them "to find themselves in something mcre suited to their interests."

And that is as it should be.

Let us talk frankly to our wife or husband or to our best friend, though we do not always recommend that either, but in the work world let us observe the courtesies and ceremonies. There is a difference between observing the ceremonies and communicating. You are not compromising your integrity by praising some egregious dumbo at his retirement. A Christmas greeting is not a communication, it is a ceremony. We quote an illustration of this from a communication book*:

> The author remembers well the annual crisis in a big cor-
> poration with which he was associated over the president's
> Christmas message to the stockholders. Every year, begin-
> ning with the Executive Vice-President and on down, we
> would take a crack at it. Our best talents would work on it,
> and the message would be hammered out, word by painful
> word, phrase by tortured phrase, until we had what we
> thought was a foolproof message. You have seen the kind. It
> had been a good year, the message would say, or, if it had
> been a bad year, we called it "a year fraught with chal-
> lenge," and the president would like to express to each and
> every one of us, and so on . . .
>
> Yet when we were done, there always seemed to be

Communicating at the Top.

something lacking, until one year, after our high-priced talent had done its painful best, one of the assistants in the author's group, a moderately talented, high-spirited chap in his late twenties, scrawled across the bottom of a second proof: *Why doesn't the bastard just say Merry Christmas?*

Of course. So much for ceremonials.

There are times, as the author points out, when telling someone off, preparing the harsh communication or laying it on the line, is beneficial and necessary both to the recipient and to the organization. At these times, if you have any integrity, you will do so. You will keep in mind also Lincoln's famous remark: "To sin by silence when they should protest makes cowards of men."

On the other hand, needless veracity ("I feel I must tell you . . ."), like malicious obedience ("I only did exactly what you asked me to do to the letter . . ."), can be extremely destructive to the recipient and to the organization.

Key principle for being frank in the work world

Ask yourself one question about any frank message you intend to deliver: What good will it do?

Being Devious

Using ceremonial language, communicating only when the communication does not harm or has some value, is one thing. Being devious or hypocritical is another.

"Bill, I wouldn't worry about it."

"What do you mean?"

"Rick Burrow's remark that you and your group are going to have to shape up or there's going to be a reorganization."

"When did he say that?"

"Yesterday. He was talking to a couple of people. I didn't see who they were but I overheard him."

"I can't imagine why he'd say that about us. We did very well in the last quarter."

"Well, maybe I heard wrong, but your name was mentioned. Just forget I said anything."

"Jack, how can I forget a remark like that? You've really got me worried."

"Just forget I said anything, Bill. I probably didn't hear right."

This kind of deviousness, whatever the purpose, serves only to disrupt an organization. Furthermore, those in the group quickly catch on to someone who is devious and label that person a troublemaker (see "Troublemaker"). He or she is quickly isolated, and eventually the organization gets rid of the troublemaker or begins to suffer disintegration.

There are other forms of deviousness in language within the work and commercial worlds too. Consider this recall letter from an automobile company: "Continued driving with a failed axle bearing could result in the disengagement of the axle shaft and adversely affect vehicle control . . ." That means the rear wheels might drop off. This sort of deviousness, while hard to take, is at least understandable since few automobile companies want to come right out and say their product is dangerous.

We have pointed out that using ceremonial language or euphemisms in the work world is not devious and may be necessary. Being courteous and considerate of others is not deviousness.

Consider, however, the dictum quoted by Edward Frank Allen of the hard-boiled editor of a well-known newspaper to his reporters:

We do not commence. We begin. We do not purchase. We buy. We do not pass away. We die. We are not all gentlemen but we are all men. Not all women are ladies, but all women are women. We do not reside in residences. We live in homes. We do not retire. We go to bed. Our priests, ministers and rabbis are not divines. Our lawyers are not barristers. Our undertakers are not morticians. Our real estate dealers are not realtors. Our plumbers are not sanitary engineers. Our cobblers are not shoe rebuilders. And the first reporter who writes a body landing "with a dull sickening thud" will land with a dull sickening thud on the street, with hat in one hand and pay envelope in the other.

Euphemisms are not a crime, but they should be used sparingly. Try not to be devious or hypocritical in act, in thought or even in language, and your relationships at the job will be on a sound basis.

Key strategies for being trusted in the work world

1. Be straightforward in your dealings with your boss, your associates, your subordinates. Where an honest response would be helpful to them and beneficial to the organization, make it.

2. Avoid using innuendo, rumor and obscure references in communicating with those you want to reach.

3. In dealing with people, use their language and use it as simply and directly as you know how.

Loner

"We used to talk about him all the time. He never went out to lunch with any of us. He never stayed for a drink afterward. Yet he was pleasant enough. He wasn't married. He didn't seem to have any friends. He got in on time. He was good at his work. He was easy enough to deal with. Once in a while we'd see him fooling around with a chess setup in his office, but you ask him to have a game and he'd smiled pleasantly and say, 'Maybe sometime.'

"He didn't seem to need anybody else. He was rather good-looking, but any time one of the girls around the office approached him except on business, he was gone. We used to wonder whether . . . well, whether he was queer, but he didn't seem so. There was no evidence of it at all. He lived alone in town. Someone went by where he lived once and said it was a very good neighborhood off Park, a very good building. He seemed to be making a good salary—research and development group. He had a nice smile. You didn't feel he was putting you off but, except for the work, you could never seem to engage him.

"Ours is a very friendly office. We all get along. Oh, there's the usual minor friction sometimes. I don't mean it was any paradise, but we knew each other, our dumbnesses, our foibles, our weaknesses. We never knew his. We never knew him at all. I guess we all liked him, but we never got to know him. He did his work and he was pleasant. And that's what makes it so . . . so, I don't know.

"Even the papers couldn't make it out. There was no reason for it.

"He had a sister out in St. Louis, and I guess she came to claim the body.

"He didn't even leave a note.

"We still talk about him."

Things to consider if you are a loner

1. If you are a loner, you will not necessarily be unpopular or resented.

2. Organizations do have jobs and support people who like to work alone and be alone.

3. There is always someone who is willing to try to understand.

Troublemaker

There are people in organizations, as in life, who are happiest when things are in turmoil, and if the place seems too quiet, they will stir things up.

> "I stood up for you, Marty."
> "What do you mean, Len?"
> "Well, when Bannerman was saying how he felt you were wrong about the Trask Project and had been wrong all along, I said you had changed your mind."
> "I was never against the Trask Project, Len. I just said we were moving too slowly."
> "You know how Bannerman is. You can never trust him. Besides, he doesn't like you so he'll say these things."
> "I don't know where he got the idea I was against the project. Actually, I was for it, Len. I'm not so sure I'm crazy about Bannerman either."
> "Well, don't tell him I tipped you off."

Len is a troublemaker.

Most jobholders catch on to the Lens after awhile and manage to avoid them. Avoiding a troublemaker, however, is not the same as being allergic to anyone who disturbs one's routine. Originals are often troublemakers in the best sense of the word: they disturb the bureaucracy with new ideas and suggestions. New ideas are disturbing and sometimes vigorously punished. Look what happened to Socrates. If you have new or original ideas, learn to handle them with care and to present them within the framework of the old routines and the conventional thinking of that organization. All organizations claim they welcome new ideas and constructive criticism. It is a mistake to take them at their word. You may end up known as a troublemaker.

Organizations need this kind of troublemaker, but he or she must understand how to introduce either original ideas or improvements of any sort. The bureaucracy knows how to handle new ideas. Here is a brief list of the way it goes about it:

"We tried that some years ago, and it didn't work."
"That's a great idea, but this is not the time for it."
"Have you checked this with our accounting people and the lawyers?"
"Why don't you talk this over with Harry Brown in Duluth, Bill Mack in Winnepeg and Stu Hunter in Hamburg?"
"I really haven't had time to think about it."
"Don't you think we have enough on our plate now?"
"There are a few thoughts of my own I want to discuss with you but not right now."
"It's a good idea. Let's form a committee and have them consider it."

If the organization has worked out a way to tolerate and deflect good ideas, it positively hates so-called constructive criticism and even bridles at "improvements." You must learn to avoid constructive criticism and to present improvements in the right way.

Let us listen to two jobholders in a major organization talking to the head of the department. One will be labeled a troublemaker. The other will be commended for his perception. Both are making the same suggestion.

"Jim, you've asked for some constructive criticism, so I'll level with you. The department really is a mess. I guess you know it as well as I do, and I suppose it isn't all your fault, but look at the way we're processing these damn vouchers. Hell, it takes forever, and

111

they're complaining about the cost, and I don't blame them. Sure, we need security but we could cut down on that stupid double-checking system you set up. Why every voucher? Why couldn't we do it only on amounts over $1,000? Your insistence on all this extra work is what slows everything up. It costs the organization about $120,000 a year, and what do we save in catching errors and fraud the way we're doing it? . . ."

Now let us hear the same suggestion in another key:

"Jim, what would you think of a way we might save about $30,000 a year by revising our voucher checking procedures and still not overlook any material irregularities? . . ."

"Let's hear it," Jim says.

Bad troublemakers disrupt an organization. Good troublemakers improve things but only if they know how to present their changes. Learn to avoid indulging yourself in "constructive criticism" on the job. Give only values, and your changes may go through.

Two thoughts about handling troublemakers

How do you handle a bad troublemaker?

1. First, learn from friends and associates who in the organization are considered troublemakers and how they go about their tricks.
2. Avoid them.

How do you go about presenting good ideas so that you are not considered a troublemaker?

1. Avoid criticizing—constructively or otherwise—no matter how urgently you are asked to make such criticisms.

2. Present the improvement only and in relation to its value and do not overlook its cost in time, effort or expense.

3. Emphasize the value specifically for the person who must make the change or implement it as well as for the organization.

Persuading

Much of your job, as you go up in your career, will consist of persuading others to follow your way of thinking or to do something you believe is in your own or the organization's best interests.

"Harry, in your presentation this afternoon, you're asking the heads of three big departments to make changes that will cost them something. In other words, you're asking them to make an investment in our new project. How are you going to present it?"

"Marty, I'm going to tell it like it is and let the chips fall where they may. Those that don't like it won't like it no matter what I say. Those that do will give us a chance—maybe. We'll go to the next level if we don't get satisfaction. Maybe we should have started there. I've learned over the years that people just can't be persuaded. They want something or they don't want it, and that's that."

"Well, Harry, with that approach, I'm afraid we're plowing the sea. If these people are behind it or at least neutral, the boss won't go against their opinions . . ."

Let us ask some questions concerning Harry's approach.
Can people be persuaded? Who can be persuaded? How can people be changed? What appeals are most effective? How are ideas put over?

All these questions have been studied by psychologists, social scientists and others, and their answers are roughly as follows:

1. Within limits, people can be persuaded, depending on how it is done, who does it and what the subject and objective is.

2. Highly persuadable are people with imagination and sensitivity. Intelligence and sensitivity—two of the characteristics of opinion leaders—open the mind to new ideas. Highly persuadable but easily counterswayed are people with low self-esteem. Resistant to persuasion are dull or hostile personalities. The extreme form of resistance to persuasion is the paranoid type. Also difficult to persuade: highly aggressive personalities and those who lack normal responsiveness.

3. The experiments on how people can be changed have centered largely on three kinds of studies: the order of presentation, the effectiveness of source and the effects of emotion. Simplified, the findings are as follows:

   a. For those already of an opinion, presenting only the favorable side is more effective. For those opposed, presenting both sides is more effective.

   b. While no difference was observed in the proportion of people who changed their minds in the direction originally advocated, whether given a one-sided or a two-sided communication, those given the two-sided communication, the opposite side first, proved to be highly resistant to the effects of a subsequent effort to change their opinion again to the contrary viewpoint, while those given only one side were not. Apparently, presenting the other side first has a certain immunizing effect against counterarguments.

c. When contradictory information is presented by one person, material presented first tends to be more credible than communications presented subsequently, but interposing some time-filling activity between the two presentations can eliminate this primary effect.

d. The influence of order of presentation is weaker on persons who are more than usually interested in the subject.

e. Placing first the communication whose contents are highly desirable to the people involved is more effective persuasion than is the reverse order.

f. When presenting arguments contrary to the position advocated, the communicator should give his own side first rather than second.

g. With regard to the influence of authority, it was found that while the prestige of the source is important in the persuasiveness of a message, this difference appears to dissipate over a period of time, and the message must then stand on its own. In these experiments, four weeks after the message was given, the content remained, but the source, whether prestigious or not, was apparently forgotten, only the content retaining its influence.

What appeals are effective?

It is well established in our folklore that people are primarily swayed by their emotions, and that if one can gain control of their attention through emotion, one can persuade. That this is just as unrealistic as the opposite supposition, namely, that people are wholly rational, is easily borne out by practically all the experiments so far made in this field.

Your own experience will tell you that generally people are rational and well aware of their own interests, that they are not to be swayed by senseless desires or passing emotions on matters of any import, and generally that such appeals are more likely to be distrusted than otherwise. Even such a powerful emotion as fear becomes ineffective if used in cataclysmic terms as shown in experiments with people on the dangers of smoking, the atom bomb, cancer, et cetera. Apparently the high fear quotient arouses strong defenses and blanks out persuasive power.

This is not to say, of course, that emotion does not have a persuasive effect, all other things being equal, but the kind of persuasion, the kind of appeal that lasts and the appeals that make their mark on important issues lie deeper than emotion or sentimentality. While the carnival barker still draws them in and the confidence man still makes his quick killing, the man who would change the thoughts and lives of others must operate at a profounder level and offer a far better quality product; first, his own sincerity and depth, second, his own substantial thought and deeply felt desire, and, finally, what is true and what will stand up without him.

How are ideas put over?

Dr. Elihu Katz, in an article on the diffusion of new ideas and practices, lists six conclusions reached from a number of experiments:

1. The influence of other people that one knows and has learned to trust is the most powerful influence in putting over an idea—more powerful than mass media or any other persuader.

2. Those who influenced others tended to be persons close to the people whom they influenced and tended to share the same social status. It was almost as rare to find someone of higher social status directly influencing someone of lower status as vice versa.

116

3. Close associates tended to hold opinions and attitudes in common and were reluctant to depart from the group consensus even where a mass appeal seemed attractive.

4. As indicated earlier, group leaders tended to specialize in the type of leadership they exerted. One would be an influence in fashion, say; another in marketing, etc.

5. Influence tended to flow from the more sensitive and aware to the less sensitive and aware until it was halted by the imperviousness of those who were completely resistant to change.

6. Those who diffused ideas—opinion leaders—were more exposed to media of all types than their followers, particularly in their own spheres of interest.

These studies appeared to show that a pattern was followed in the diffusion of an idea or an innovation. The pattern showed three stages: (1) the idea is presented or the innovation tried out by a small number of "advanced" or cosmopolitan persons who have picked up the idea or innovation in their reading and listening and who, having tried the idea or innovation out, pass it on to their friends and followers; (2) in the second stage it spreads fast because of obvious advantages and the tides of fashion; and (3) in the last stage it becomes the norm, and the older, more isolated members of the group reluctantly take it up.

One basic and paramount principle seemed to hold in putting over any new idea: not only must it be accepted by the opinion leaders, but it must fit into the framework of the culture, and if it is a real innovation, it must somehow be channeled into the prevailing value system of society. All ideas or changes to secure acceptance must somehow be made compatible with the prevailing patterns of ideas and, in order to conform, must often be initially modified.

117

Some basic techniques to consider in persuading people

1. Find and identify the values you have to offer.

2. Study those you wish to persuade, assess their amenability to persuasion, consider the order of presentation of your message, consider the receptivity of the message in relation to you as the sender. Should you or someone else propose it?

3. In all persuasion, the most effective appeal is self-interest—the value to the listener of your message as well as the overall value to the organization. The overall value to the organization may not be enough. It is difficult to persuade someone to do something no matter how much it may benefit the organization or others if it is not in his or her self-interest. Find where the listener's self-interest lies.

4. Work out what appeal in the communication will prove most effective and valuable and begin with that appeal.

The Killer Boss

Most of us are fairly lucky with the people we report to in our jobs, but in almost every career a time comes when we may find ourselves stuck behind a stupid or sometimes malicious boss.

"Did you see what he did this time?"

"No, what happened?"

"You know that marketing program I worked so hard on that he told me was something they'd tried before and had turned out to be a complete failure?"

"Yes, I remember your showing it to me. It looked pretty good. I don't remember their ever trying anything like that, Harvey. I thought it was brilliant."

"Well, apparently it was. It seems Old Dumbo de-

118

cided to present it after all to the committee. He presented it as his own, and he's basking in the glory at the moment. The pilot was a great success. They're budgeting for it. My name wasn't mentioned."

"My God!"

"Well, that's the way the cookie crumbles with that guy."

This kind of boss seems to have adopted literally the cynical definition of an executive: "A person who takes all the credit, avoids all the work and shifts all the blame."

Techniques, tactics and stratagems in handling the killer boss

Advice in such situations is hard to come by unless you can quit. The most frequent advice is to ask for a transfer. Both stupidity and maliciousness are hard to combat. The problem is avoiding the vengeance of Dumbo. Dumb bosses can be awfully smart when their reputations are at stake. They know all about end runs, transfers, letting it be known and protests.

End runs. One of the main problems of advancing in a career is exposure. How do you get the people upstairs to know you? Good bosses, of course, showcase their best people. Top management is always saying they judge a manager in part by the people he brings along, but with Dumbo the quickest way to bring on repressive measures is to be praised by someone upstairs. Dumbo usually counters with, "Yes, he's doing better now but it was touch and go for awhile. And I'm afraid he's not out of the woods yet. . . ." It is always difficult and sometimes dangerous to try an end run with an idea. The response usually is, "Have you checked this with Mr. D?" And Old Dumbo has you again.

Transfers. This may be the essential move. The technique is to request the transfer to broaden yourself. You need experience, you say, in marketing (if you are in plant engineering) or in an operating job (if you are in a staff position). Never, however, under any circumstances let it out that there is a "personality conflict" or that you can't work for Old Dumbo or that he's gored you just one time too many. You must get out of there clean. Dumbo may some day tell his people that he gave you your start, that he pushed you out into that larger world.

Letting it be known. Again, this may be counterproductive. Higher management doesn't want any trouble. They don't want to know that you and your boss don't get along or that he is doing to you what he does to all promising people reporting to him. Let someone else bring it to their attention. Eventually they will catch on, but meanwhile, if you let it be known, you will be smeared with the "trouble" down there. Get out as fast and as cleanly as you can, unless you have decided to leave. In that case you will be doing the company a favor to let them know they have someone who will guarantee that no promising individual ever gets past him. Some exit comments can save the organization a lot of grief.

Protesting. You will be labeled a troublemaker. Unless you are leaving or have independent means; then see above under "Letting it be known."

What is important, however, is not to give way to despair, to realize this is a temporary situation and others will eventually catch on to Dumbo's tactics.

Most Dumbos unfortunately are sincere. They honestly believe they taught their people everything they know. They have what has come to be known as a "my people" syndrome. They honestly believe they had the ideas or developed the projects they stole. They feel it is their right to take credit for anything good that comes from their department, but for the good of the department to avoid blame for any of their own stupidities or disasters. They believe they serve as an honest but strict father and that credit does belong to them.

They also need to compensate for lack of talent or brains, and their insecurity can make them extremely dangerous.

One warning we have been asked to give: Are you sure the person is as stupid and unfair as you think? Can it be that you are a victim of your own insecurities? Is it possible that you yourself are suffering from paranoia (see "He's out to get me")? Be sure first; then protect yourself.

Why Doesn't He/She Like Me?

While it may seem almost inconceivable that anyone would not like us, in the work world it is sometimes brought to our attention that we may be actively disliked by someone.

There may be several reasons for this, some of them puzzling since we started out being liked or we would not have been hired. If you are in this position, here are some points to ponder:

First, you may have done something outstanding that disturbed the routine or procedures of the group.

Second, as has been pointed out, you may be in a supervisory position and do good work that in itself can ensure equivocal feelings toward you.

Third, you may unwittingly have made someone else look bad, thus putting his or her job in jeopardy or at least increasing the person's feeling of insecurity.

Fourth, you may be insensitive to a political situation in which you are the supporter of one side and those on the other side consider you an enemy.

Fifth, you may be a good executive and have had to make a hard choice that of necessity has hurt someone or some group. You cannot always win popularity contests if you are in an executive position and do your job right. As someone remarked, "If you need love in your job, go into the dog-breeding business."

Sixth, you may have compounded the crime of being intelligent and able by being a woman, and there are sometimes men and even women in the organization who do not like able women.

Seventh, someone may just have the bad taste to dislike you.

Eighth, it is possible that you are mistaken and that he/she does not dislike you or simply feels neutral about you.

Finally, you may not be liked simply because you are obnoxious. If this is the case, it is worth trying to mend your manners and modify your behavior, because without a sound relationship with most of your associates, based at least on respect, you will be powerless and cannot do your job.

He's Out to Get Me

"And then you know what he did?"
"What?"
"He failed to send me the memo with the figures, so when I went into the meeting, I looked like a fool. Everybody else had the costs. He had sent the memo to everyone else and given me an earlier estimate, so when I tried to give that estimate, they looked puzzled and said Gorman's figures didn't jibe with mine—had I found a way to do it cheaper?"
"What did Gorman say when you confronted him?"
"He said it must have been an oversight. I was on the list to receive the memo. I really don't believe him. I think he's out to get me."

Paranoia?
It is hard to know sometimes.
Most organizations are not hotbeds of people trying to undermine each other. Still, there are ploys the devious or the malevolent sometimes use to embarrass or undermine objects of their dislike.

122

Three tactics and strategies that have been used to undermine people

Withholding essential information: What you don't know in any job or any organization can hurt you. And you need all the information you can get. There has been a lot of commentary recently on information overload and receiving information on a "need to know" basis. Managers generally complain they get too much information; those reporting to them feel they get too little. You would do well to see that in your job you receive all essential information from whatever source and that you are plugged into the grapevine and know what is going on. One of the ploys of the malicious is to withhold or divert essential information or to disseminate misleading information.

Downgrading the victim to his superior: This can be extremely harmful when done skillfully. Implying reluctance to let out something derogatory, damning with faint praise, praising with a bad kicker at the end—all can prove devastating under certain circumstances.

"He's a great guy, Jim. I only wish he weren't so careless. He's really costing us some problems with our customers." (This to a meticulous boss.)

"I can't explain how he got into that mess, Al. Oh, I thought you knew. I'm really sorry. It was nothing. Forget I ever mentioned it. It was personal. I don't want to say anymore." (To a straitlaced, conventional executive.)

Sabotaging a project: This type of "getting someone" is often perpetrated on an executive who has angered the bureaucracy. It consists of three types of ploys: (a) malicious obedience, (b) imbecilic goodwill and (c) selective amnesia.

In *malicious obedience,* the perpetrator appears to be overtaken with a sudden tragic loss of even rudimentary common sense. "But you told me you wanted to look at a few examples," Jack Conran says, dumping a ton of computer readouts on the victim's desk. "I didn't know you wanted them edited out and only two or three. I can't read your mind. I was trying to do exactly what you asked me to do. This is a group of only 107 examples—that's what took me so long."

In *imbecilic goodwill,* the perpetrator comes in with something completely irrelevant to the project after you have pleaded with him to hurry up on an assignment. You look at him and say, "But Jack, what has that to do with what I assigned you to get?" And Jack looks hurt and says in a harried, crestfallen voice, "I thought this would interest you, Al. We're only doing our best."

In *selective amnesia,* the perpetrator remembers everything but the most important part of the assignment for the project. He keeps coming in with some nonessential detail here and there, and when you say, "That's all very well, Jack, but how about the figures for the whole project," he says, "We're working on them, Al. They're coming along, but here's the cost estimates for the sidearms . . ."

Most organizations, despite folklore, are not jungles. Most jobholders do their best and try to play fair in their relationships. Still, at some time in your career, you may come upon one of these sharks, who for whatever reason is out to get you. If you are good and do your job, the odds are greatly in your favor that you will survive such a person. The organization catches on to people like these quickly and usually can eliminate them or render them harmless before they do too much damage.

Techniques, tactics and strategies to consider in protecting yourself

Perhaps the most effective remedy for the ploys described is exposure. You must collect the evidence of this sort of maliciousness, confront the perpetrator and explain what happened both to those around you and to your superior. The evidence must be concrete and specific. It must be presented unemotionally. Your reputation and your work will then stand as witnesses for you.

1. Identify which malicious stratagem is being used on you.

2. Collect evidence—exact events or any documentation possible.

3. Consider whether to confront the perpetrator first and whether this will put a stop to it.

4. Explain what seems to be happening to friendly associates and ask their advice.

5. If this does not put a stop to it, go to your superior and explain the problem unemotionally. It is important to protect your reputation and your work.

6. Finally, be fair yourself. Do not become one of those out to get someone.

Mentor

"Now that you've been elected chairman, John," one of the directors, an old friend, is saying, "how are you going to celebrate before the big party tonight?"

"I'm going to see Mr. Carruthers," the new chairman answered.

"Old Charlie Carruthers!" the director said. "Why he must have retired ten years ago. Why are you going to see him?"

"Well, Arthur," the chairman said, "old Mr. Carruthers—I still can't call him Charlie—was my mentor when I first started here twenty years ago. I learned what the world was like from him. He was my boss's boss but he took an interest in me and brought me along. He opened up horizons for me. I wouldn't be where I am today if it weren't for him."

"Good Lord, John, I remember Old Charlie—he

was a crusty old son of a bitch, though he did have a flair. So he brought you along.''

"Yes, I was a greenhorn. I didn't know much but I thought I knew everything. Mr. Carruthers liked me. He was like a father to me. I learned about the company and even a bit about life from him. I'm going to see him this afternoon before the party tonight. He should be there, but he won't come. You fellows wouldn't be giving me this party if it weren't for him . . .''

Most of those—some say all of those—who have succeeded and reached high places in an organization have had a mentor, someone whom they admired and from whom they learned, someone who took an interest in them and brought them along. In some organizations he may be called a godfather; in others a rabbi; or if a woman, mother. But the truth is if you are to succeed and to go up in any organization, you need a mentor. Listen to the voice of Dr. Harry Levinson of the Levinson Institute of Cambridge, Massachusetts: "Why don't people make it without mentors? The reasons are simple. All organizations necessarily must be political. That is, they are made up of individuals and groups of people who need each other's help to get their work done.''

Most of the work of an organization is done through informal associations—networks—and unless you can somehow through the influence of someone important plug into the organization network, you will find it hard not only to get anything done but also to progress in the organization and in your career.

Your mentor may be your boss or he or she may be some other influential person in the organization whom you admire and who takes an interest in you and helps bring you along. You learn through your mentor; you may learn about life and the world as well as about the organization and how to operate in it.

All of us need a mentor at some time in our career. The best mentors take pleasure in bringing along, protecting and cherishing those they like. There are people who desire only followers and will only bring you along if you obey them implicitly, pander to their prejudices, aid them in their ambitions or meet their demands for popularity. These are not true mentors, and you should beware of them.

Women in organizations particularly need mentors, because in most male-dominated organizations they have less access to the power network and less opportunity to learn what is going on through outside informal channels. A danger arises, of course, because a male-female relationship can be misinterpreted. Yet few women, according to the international executive recruiter John Wareham, have made it to a high position in the business world without a mentor.

Mentors are teachers, guides, builders and enrichers of people. As you go up in your career and become influential and an opinion leader, you can have no more meaningful and gratifying experience than becoming yourself a mentor to some promising younger person.

How to find a mentor

1. Identify opinion leaders in and out of the organization and seek them out (see "Opinion Leaders").

2. Within the organization, try to find someone you admire, go to him or her and ask for guidance and counsel on a specific project that might interest that person.

3. Further, try to find someone you admire in your field or type of work either in or outside the organization, go to him or her and ask for guidance and counsel on a specific project.

4. Continue the search until you find someone who will take an interest in you personally and in your career.

The Grapevine

What is the grapevine and how do you plug into it?

In the work world, the grapevine is the rumor mill, and yet as part of the vast sea of informal communicating in any organization, it has a larger impact than any of the formal communication channels. People call it scuttlebutt or "what they are saying," and some managers tend to dismiss it as generally wrong and trivial stuff that should not be listened to. This is a serious mistake.

In a closed organization, that is, an organization with few formal channels of communication and where a "need to know" basis for communicating is the norm, the grapevine virtually runs the organization. Even in the most open kind of organization, with many channels of communication, the grapevine plays a powerful role. Anyone who expects to have any influence in an organization must learn to plug into the grapevine.

What kind of material travels the grapevine?
All kinds.
Who likes whom.
Who is going up.
Who is going down.
How people feel about so-and-so.
What office romances are taking place.
What terrible thing the organization is contemplating for its
    people.
Why so-and-so left the company.
Who has a drinking problem.
Why the Brender Project was aborted.
Who got a raise and why.
Who has the influence.
How we are doing this year.
Why there will be no office party this year.

What took place in the board meeting.
What the survey of employees really brought out.
How many people are going to be fired.
Whether the company is going to be acquired and by which company.

Literally hundreds of items of vital interest to those in the organization travel the grapevine.

How much of what you hear by the grapevine is true? That depends. Not all of it, of course, is true, and sometimes it can be wholly wrong. This was described in the case of a manager in a large food company who expected to be promoted to a long-sought higher position. He heard by the grapevine that others were being considered for the promotion and decided he was being passed over. He could not face this and decided to go to another job. He went in a week later to tell his boss he was quitting.

"But why, Jim?" his boss said, "We were just about to offer you this big promotion—a job I thought you always wanted—to head this division."

"But you were interviewing others for the job, I heard," Jim said.

"We were interviewing others to replace you when you were promoted," the vice-president replied. "I don't know where you got the idea we would consider anyone else."

Nevertheless, the grapevine is right a large part of the time and, even more important, it reflects the opinions, the fears, the hopes, the anxieties of those working in the organization, and those who hope to know what is going on must somehow learn to plug into it. Regardless of your job or your position, if you are not part of the grapevine, you will find you are powerless.

129

Techniques for plugging into the grapevine

1. *Get out of your office or workplace and move around.* You will never hear anything sitting quietly in an office or working in one spot.

2. *Identify the opinion leaders and the gossips.* Sometimes the same person may be both. Opinion leaders (see "Opinion Leaders") are more sensitive to what is going on than others. They also tend to influence the course of events wherever they are. The gossips are good transmitters of the more "interesting" and personal aspects of organization life. Many persons say "I never listen to gossip." This is a mistake. The grapevine carries an enormous store of gossip. If you don't listen, you won't know what's going on.

3. *Become trusted.* To get information, you must give information. And it must be sound information. If you use the grapevine only to "get" someone or to start baseless rumors, you will become known as a troublemaker and as someone not to be trusted. And you will find the grapevine passes you by—no one tells you anything. To enter the grapevine you must be trusted.

4. *Keep circulating and listen.* Build friendships. Come on as a person, not as an employee or a manager or someone out to get something. The flow never ceases. The grapevine operates twenty-four hours a day, seven days a week. An organization is a huge community and like any community, there is a continuing back-fence gossip. If you want to hear it, you must get out where it is going on; you must circulate and become part of the network.

The grapevine will tell you where it's at.

Managing Up

In any job, your relationship with your boss is a survival matter. The problem is that many jobholders have such an

130

ambivalent or resentful feeling about this dependency relationship that they fail to look at the relationship at all or to handle it with the care and interest it deserves.

To most of us, authority figures of any sort may arouse feelings that are often rebellious and angry even though suitably masked. Most of us rebel at some time during our life, usually at adolescence, against our families, particularly our parents. We need and we wish for what we term independence, and this very natural and healthy desire is carried into our adult world.

The sailor dreams of the little chicken farm he will retire to, the bureaucrat of the little business of his own he will start, but meanwhile we live in a world where we are not independent in the sense we may dream about, and we report to others in our jobs.

So it is important to understand and manage the reporting relationship. It is important to see the relationship for what it is, without the emotional overtones. If you are a healthy person, your ego will not be destroyed every time you are ordered to do something you may not want to do. You may be saddened but you are not overwhelmed by your boss's stupidity and intransigence. You have learned both the value and the defects of the relationship and, knowing your own worth and value, you are able to look at your relationship with your superiors as something to be managed with sympathy and care just as they must look at their relationship with you and others who report to them.

Techniques, tactics and strategies in managing up

1. Deal with your boss with the same care and objectivity that you deal with your associates and subordinates. You try to be a friend within the bounds of the relationship.

2. "Manage" your boss in the same way you manage your other relationships and your job. Try to understand your boss as a person. Try to understand what his or her job

131

entails and what demands and pressures it engenders. Try to understand and accommodate yourself to the boss's style of supervising. If your boss is a woman, she may need even more your understanding and sympathetic support in a male-dominated corporate culture.

3. Try to maintain communication with your boss and discuss problems that can affect him or her so that your boss is not surprised or unprepared for any consequences of problems you may meet. Do not, however, use up the boss's time on trivial or nonessential matters. The boss's time is as limited and heavily allocated as your own.

4. Look at the boss's operations as you would look at your own. You should understand the planning, communicating, organizing, administering and controlling that must be put into the area as a whole for which he or she is responsible.

5. If the boss is difficult or you have problems in dealing with each other, analyze the way he or she is coming to you—as a parent, an adult or a child (see "Supervisory Styles") and consider how you can relate to your boss most effectively. See also "The Killer Boss" and "He's Out to Get Me" on ways to protect yourself.

Opinion Leaders

Every organization has certain people who influence the way those in the organization think and whose opinions carry special weight. Sociologists call them opinion leaders, and they are the people it is well to get to know if you want to put over any important project.

These people may be found in any part of the organization, not necessarily at the top. A secretary can be an opinion leader and so may a warehouse foreman. You yourself may become an opinion leader.

In earlier societies, the world of power, of opinion and taste leaders, of those who counted, was known as the Great World. That was where a person had to turn to get anything done or to put across any important enterprise. That was where the leaders were. This Great World had its power centers in the courts of kings and the great capitals of Europe. Its principals were generally known to each other and they were generally born to the rights and privileges of the Great World, although remarkable abilities and achievements, such as those of great artists and thinkers, great military leaders and fantastic personalities, might gain entry. This was the Establishment when our Western society was younger. In today's society leadership is very widespread and diverse, and it comprises not a tiny caste of privileged men who through birth and tradition dominate the prestige, the goods and the activities of society but a broad spectrum of people in every walk of life, relatively few of whom are known to each other and who exercise their influence in a myriad of different ways. Sociologists have estimated that some 20 percent of those in an open society like ours can be ranked as opinion leaders. And in an organization, opinion leaders may comprise some 20 percent of the total personnel.

Who are these opinion leaders and how can they be reached?

Here is a summary, from a book on communicating, of what is known about opinion leaders:

> Sociologists and those interested for commercial reasons have during the last few years spent some time studying the so-called opinion and taste leader in our society. These studies were originally triggered by the finding that mass media do not work either as directly or as simply as had been supposed on the mass audience to which they are beamed; that, in fact, they have surprisingly little effect unless supplemented or reinforced by climate of opinion and personal influence.
>
> These findings should not perhaps have been so surpris-

ing. People are influenced more by people, by the full power of the tangible personality, than by disembodied voices, or shadows on a screen, or printed words or screaming banners. They are influenced by those they admire or trust, by those who seem to them experts or authorities, by those whose disinterestedness they are sure of, and by the casual word, the aside, the tentative remark thrown away, far more than by the great, booming, pounding sea of advertising and blather, no matter how impressive or skillfully produced . . .

It was also found that all opinion and taste leaders shared three key characteristics which gave them their status and influence: (1) They were, as might be imagined, in sensitive positions which were regarded as giving them special competence in the field in which they influenced people. (2) They were unusually well informed; they read more, listened to the mass media more, were more sensitive to the tides of fashion and change; they knew more people, were more gregarious, and particularly, they communicated more. Finally, (3) they cared; they showed a much higher degree of real interest and warmth toward their subjects, were much more likely to have cherished opinions and to have developed cherished tastes; and they gave more of themselves to whatever they became interested in.

It is perhaps not too astonishing that these three qualities appeared in almost every case of an opinion or taste leader. They might well have been deduced from man's long experience with those who have influenced him most through the years, but it is comforting to know that the sociological findings fully support them as characteristics. It is also worth knowing that to reach the rest, it is important to reach first these leaders.

Techniques and strategies in finding and dealing with opinion leaders

1. Ask your associates who are the "authorities" in various fields. You ask them who people go to for help in various

areas. These persons are apt to be the opinion leaders. You also look around and see which people are involved in the most activities in the organization and which are said to have distinguished themselves in various ways.

2. Select those you intend to approach and find out every-thing you can about them—their interests, their activities, their background, where they have lunch, who they eat with and their routines.

3. Approach them on some specific project or activity within the scope of their leadership. You will generally find that although they may be the busiest people, they tend to be the most helpful and the quickest to respond. They also are likely to deal with other opinion leaders in getting projects through.

4. Through developing relationships with opinion leaders, you move into a power network that can help you with any projects you would like to put over. Opinion leaders like to be consulted. They tend to know what's going on and can assess the implications of projects or programs. Anything they support is apt to go through. Things they oppose are apt not to go through.

Loyalty

Loyalty is caring.

It is not necessarily agreeing with everything the organization does. It is not necessarily loving the organization. It is not necessarily following every policy or procedure or order the organization sets down. But it is caring about the organization—wanting it to succeed, to prosper, to have a good future and a good name.

While this caring, this loyalty may, and in normal people usually does, have a large component of self-interest in it—after all your livelihood depends on the survival and profitabil-ity of the organization—that does not detract one whit from the value and necessity of loyalty.

The problem may arise with higher management's definition of what loyalty is or, more important, with what those in responsible positions consider being disloyal. Criticizing certain company policies has in some organizations been considered disloyal. Revealing serious defects in certain operations has been considered disloyal, and blowing the whistle on illegal acts by persons in an organization has been considered disloyal (see Part IV, "The Outside Work World").

That is not to say that there is no way to be disloyal to an organization. The most common forms of disloyalty may be grouped under acts in four areas:

Subverting discipline and morale
Revealing the organization's proprietary confidential information or operations
Harming the organization or its management through gratuitous public statements
Conflicts of interest

Subverting discipline and morale

Troublemaking and politicking in an organization can become active disloyalty to the organization or its management when it reaches the stage of disruption of legitimate authority or to a degree deliberately destroys a group's morale. You may deeply resent certain aspects of the organization's administration or certain of its people, but there are legitimate ways of presenting your opinions. You become disloyal when you use tactics that destroy the legitimate discipline an organization must impose in order to function or when you undermine morale to the point where the group cannot function in an acceptable manner.

Revealing the organization's proprietary and confidential information or operations

Every organization builds up through hard work and talent proprietary information and developments that give it an ad-

136

vantage over its competitors in the marketplace. In high-technology companies, this proprietary information, known to many of its people who have access to it or have helped develop it, is of great monetary value. There may also be other information the company does not want revealed—future plans, new directions, special programs. If you are privy to this special information, it is an act of disloyalty to reveal it to unauthorized sources. In extreme cases, of course, you may be prosecuted for actually selling technological material that belongs to the company, but we are speaking here of that gray area where revealing confidential information is not a crime but nevertheless can harm the company. This is an act of disloyalty.

Harming the organization or its management through gratuitous public statements

Here again it is perfectly legitimate to criticize certain aspects of the organization or of its personnel, if done privately. This may even be an act of loyalty, since it may show that you care for the organization, its future and its good name. However, if you are in a position to harm the organization's reputation by your public statements, such statements while you are a member of the organization can be considered an act of disloyalty.

Conflicts of interest

A conflict of interest may be defined as placing self-interest before your duty or loyalty to those who have hired you. Using this definition, the following are common areas where conflicts of interest have occurred:

—The jobholder who is in a position to profit personally from a decision he makes in behalf of the company, as in taking a kickback or special favor from a supplier.

137

—The corporate manager or officer who is in a position to profit personally from the use of inside information as in buying or selling his own stock before significant news about the company is released to the public.

—The bank loan officer who has access to information that could make—or lose—millions for the bank's trust department.

—The official who enters government service from having represented some special interest and is in a position to influence regulation of that interest or who enters a private industry he has regulated.

There are other areas of conflict of interest also, the key element being a conflict between one's own interests and profit and that of the organization one has agreed to serve. When you are placed in a position of authority and trust in an organization, you may find yourself in a position where conflict of interest can occur. Conflict of interest is one area of disloyalty that may be harmful to the organization.

Loyalty, however, does not mean subservience. As pointed out, it does not mean necessarily agreeing with everything the organization or its management does. It does not mean blind obedience to rules or policies.

It simply means caring.

Things to understand about loyalty and being loyal

1. Understand the real meaning of loyalty and do not underrate it or regard it as a lack of individuality or independence.

2. Do not use your influence or authority to subvert the organization's discipline or morale (see ''Morale'').

3. Respect the organization's proprietary confidential information or operations.

4. Consider whether public statements you may make can harm the organization.

5. Many organizations have policy statements regarding what they consider conflicts of interest. Ask to see such statements and in situations where you are not sure whether you may have a conflict of interest, consult some authority in the company.

6. Be loyal. It is not only to your interest; it is important to your integrity and to the trust placed in you.

Morale

The term *morale* is used rather loosely as meaning both high motivation and high satisfaction with the work and it is usually applied to a group or an organization rather than to an individual. The jobholder in a high-morale group will usually have high morale; that is, he will be highly motivated and feel great satisfaction with the enterprise. He will feel proud to be associated with that group and that organization and he will therefore care for it and be loyal to its interests.

Low-morale groups are subject to all the ills of dissatisfaction, dissension and ultimately disorganization. Members may through resentment or frustration sabotage the operations or sink into apathy or finally depart from the organization. At the least a low-morale organization will not be able to attract the best people or the best workers.

What then does morale consist of and how is it acquired?

Industrial psychologists have pondered the morale question, generally with regard to increasing productivity, though experiments seem to give in some cases an equivocal answer on the relationship between high productivity and high morale. What they do seem to show is that high-morale groups receive higher support, more privileges, attract better workers and, depending on the goal to be reached, more often reach their goals. Low-morale groups can have high produc-

139

tivity for short periods based on fear and heavy authoritarian pressure. High-morale groups may have high productivity when that is perceived as the specific goal, particularly in competitive relationships with other groups.

Members of a high-morale group know each other and are supportive of each other's work. Jan Berkhout, an industrial psychologist at the University of South Dakota, has described these elements and characteristics of high-morale groups:

> High morale groups are always associated with some tangible goal. In a military context the goal may be the capture of territory, the destruction of a certain number of enemy units, or the completion of a certain number of missions. In desperate situations the goal may simply be to hold a position for a certain number of days. In competitive athletics the goal is typically a championship or record, but may also be merely the bettering of some previous status. In industrial contexts, goals are generally production or sales totals, but may also be efficiency targets such as cost control, or energy use reduction, or even such intangibles as market share. Whatever the situation, these goals will have certain features in common:
>
> 1. The goals are universally perceived as both attainable and worthwhile. An occasional scoffer can be rejected from the group, but reservations about worth and attainability by more than a very few will effectively destroy the high morale situation.
>
> 2. The group perceives progress towards the goal as being both steady and tangible.
>
> 3. The attainment of the goal cannot be too far in the future . . .*

It will come as no surprise that when an organization is doing poorly or for some reason—disclosure of a major irreg-

* *Personnel Journal*, March 1982.

ularity or a public scandal or bad publicity—has fallen in public esteem, morale declines. Morale may also be destroyed by politicking, malicious rumor and gossip and bad management (see "Troublemaker," "He's out to Get Me" and "The Killer Boss").

The key to high morale is pride and good management. The good manager, who maintains a positive spirit, communicates freely and constantly his own spirit and courage, sets proper, attainable goals and shows respect for the members of his group and for the work, will be able to maintain morale under all circumstances.

In any job, you should observe and try to become associated with a high-morale group. If through the luck of the draw you find yourself in a group with low morale, there may not be much you can do about it at the moment, but consider the following:

Techniques for keeping morale high

1. Do not join in the criticism and derogation that are characteristic of low-morale groups.

2. Try to remain as cheerful and hardworking as possible.

3. Talk it up when you can. Keep a sense of humor and attach yourself to those members of the group who have a positive attitude.

Sexual Harassment

"Susan," Tom Crandal, her boss, said, "I'm very impressed with you and your abilities and I'd like to talk over our mutual interests. I'm sure your husband will understand if we have dinner together Thursday."

"He wouldn't understand, Tom. I'm sorry."

"I'm sorry too, Susan. I guess the plans on the job I had for you will have to go by the board."

"That's not fair, Tom."
"That's the way it is, Susan."

Tom's proposition is sexual harassment, and it is action-able. The organization cannot tolerate this type of pressure on an employee. The identification of sexual harassment, the pressure on people, particularly women, for sexual favors as a requirement for advancement or simply job security has been a long time coming. There has been a good deal of joking about it, articles like "Sexual Harassment—How Do I Get It?" and so on, but it is a serious matter, a form of pressure no organization can now afford to overlook or condone.

This is not to say that office romances may not spring up between consenting adults, in which no sexual harassment is involved, but like other forms of pressure or discrimination based on sex, color or creed, you are protected against, and have remedies for, sexual harassment on the job (see Part V, "Legal Remedies").

Even if the overtures are not as blatant as Tom Crandal's, the courts and society in general are introducing less obvious behavior as verging on sexual harassment, when unwelcome: forms of psychological coercion, physical contact, gestures, comments, innuendo and jokes of a sexual nature that are offensive to the victim.

Techniques, tactics and strategies in protecting yourself from sexual harassment*

1. If you find yourself working with someone who puts this kind of pressure on you, be clear, firm and polite that you are bothered by this behavior. Be diplomatic. Do not threaten or become abusive yourself.

2. At the same time, protect yourself against countercharges

* See also "Sexual Harassment: No Joking Matter," *Manager*, published by Southwestern Bell.

of complicity. Do not let it appear that you enjoy or might reciprocate the advances or that you are willing to invite such inappropriate attentions. Do not confide the intimate details of your private life or recount marital troubles to someone who might put this type of pressure on you. Avoid excessive after-hours socializing with the trouble-maker unless you are in a group.

3. Be professional in your dealings with such a person. Make it clear that you are totally involved in your job. Let the person know through your actions that you will not welcome any form of sexual harassment.

4. If the situation persists, talk to your supervisor about it or, if this is not possible, talk to personnel or to someone higher in authority in the company. If you receive no satisfaction, then talk to someone who deals with affirmative action in your state or city. You will receive confidential assistance, and your case will be investigated.

5. If the investigation reveals sexual harassment, corrective action will be taken by the agency.

Office Romance

In the work world as in life, romance, licit or illicit, occurs in almost every organization of any size. Despite the many instances of scandal occasioned by office romance, it is not a crime, and most organizations do their best to avoid any involvement in such attachments, which they rightly believe, if discretion is shown and the proprieties observed, is a private matter and not their business.

Where, as in a recent celebrated case, the president of an organization promoted an extremely able woman with whom he was rumored to be having an affair, the scandal revolved around the appearance of a conflict of interest on whether the promotion was based on her abilities or on his attachment to her. Such difficulties are perhaps inevitable when the romance affects the personnel conventions of the organization and goes against our society's moral code.

In another well-known organization, a vice-president was involved in a highly publicized scandal when his wife sued him for divorce on grounds of adultery and the suit was written about in the papers of the city in which he was located. The worldwide organization that he had been faithfully serving for many years did not discharge him for this unfortunate revelation but, not wanting to seem to condone what society considers an impropriety, very sensibly found he could best serve their interests abroad, and he found himself transferred to Caracas.

The problem with office romances, where they happen to be adulterous, is that they are extremely difficult to conceal. The grapevine operates twenty-four hours a day, and it is the rare office romance that is not known at least to the group in which it occurs. People who work together usually form a bond and often become close friends. A marriageable man and woman working together have a priori so much in common that it is not surprising if their work relationship and proximity blossom into romance. When marriage occurs, however, husband and wife are usually not permitted to work in the same department in most large organizations.

In cases where the situation becomes of great concern to management, however, it is more often the woman who is transferred or somehow induced to leave. Love is still not an equal opportunity employer.

On the other hand, the days of the office Lothario and the harassing boss who exert pressure on women associates for sexual favors are about over, since sexual harassment has finally been recognized as a form of blackmail that is actionable and that the organization is required to prevent (see "Sexual Harassment").

The office romance, however, will probably never die. Love cannot be "managed" and is not susceptible to edicts of the policy committee.

If You Are a Woman . . .

Enough has been said and written about the role of women in the work world to enable you to realize that our society is still not an equal opportunity employer where women are concerned.

Even though enormous strides have been made in the last ten years and even though women now constitute more than half of our work force, the role of women in the work world is generally less secure and less rewarding than that of men. Our society is male-oriented and male-dominated, and this is reflected in the work world as in most of our institutions. So if you are a woman, while you may because of talent and temperament have a career in all respects as fulfilling as any man's, you will have a harder row to hoe than your male counterpart in achieving it.

This does not necessarily mean that there is any overt effort in most organizations or in the work world to keep you down, but social customs and assumptions that favor males change slowly. It is still the case in our society for the male to be considered the breadwinner and favored in that role and the female to be considered the homemaker and favored in that role, and while our society is consciously making an effort to modify this orientation to provide equal opportunity in the work world for women, subconsciously many of the old habits and institutional setups favoring males still persist.

Perhaps a recent study of executive women, made by the University of California Graduate School of Business and the Korn/Ferry International executive search firm will highlight the situation and problems of women in the work world. The subjects of the study were women who had succeeded to high positions. The study was based on three hundred responses to six hundred questionnaires mailed to women at the levels of vice-president and above at the top one thousand industrial concerns on *Fortune*'s list and at three hundred of the largest companies in specialized areas. Most of the respondents were vice-presidents; their average age was forty-six, their average salaries $92,000. Their occupations ranged from corporate secretary to chief executive officer.

Here are excerpts of the findings and other studies on women as reported by Jennifer Bingham Hull in the *Wall Street Journal*:

Asked whether "barriers to women have fallen at the senior management level," 63% of the women say no. And 70% say women don't receive equal pay for comparable jobs. Female executives most frequently mention "being a woman" as their major career obstacle, citing "the old-boy network," "insecure men," and the attitude that they're "too good looking to take seriously . . . will run off and get married" as work-place problems.

In comments on her questionnaire, a vice-president of corporate finance says her biggest career obstacle has been her appearance. I "didn't look or sound the part—5'3½", female, with a Southern accent," she says. A vice-president and director of manpower development complains of "lack of acceptance based on competence . . . the unwillingness of people to give me the toughest assignments." And a regional vice-president says her biggest barrier to success has been her "tendency to unconsciously intimidate male superiors."

After "being a woman," lack of confidence was most frequently cited as the main obstacle to success. A senior vice-president of marketing says she was forced to overcome "my own fears of not being as good or strong as the men I worked with because of lack of education and being the first woman." Asked to name her greatest career challenge, another woman simply responded, "myself."

These comments sound familiar to Barbara Franklin, a senior fellow of public management of the University of Pennsylvania's Wharton School. She serves on the boards of Dow Chemical Co., Westinghouse Electric Corp., and Aetna Life & Casualty Co. Miss Franklin cites isolation and upbringing as reasons for insecurity. "Women aren't brought up with

146

male egos. And . . . in the corporate scene nobody tells you when you've done a good job. There's just this deafening silence.''

Lack of confidence, Miss Franklin says, comes from corporate women's inability to break into men's informal networks. "I see it now. Everybody I know plays golf. I don't play golf.''

The study by Korn/Ferry and UCLA follows a similar survey done in 1979. Then, the researchers set out to analyze the characteristics of senior executives, surveying about 1,700 people in senior positions below the level of chief executive officer at *Fortune*'s top 500 companies and the 300 more specialized concerns. When 99% of the respondents turned out to be men, the researchers decided to survey executive women and compare the two groups. Presidents, chief executive officers and chief operating officers were included in the female study in order to get a sufficient sample. The average age of the men surveyed was 53.

Comparison shows the biggest difference between executive men and women to be marital and family status. Fifty-two percent of the women surveyed are single, compared with only 4% of the men. In addition, 61% of the women are childless, while 97% of the men were parents.

Executive women are far more likely to be divorced than their male counterparts. Of the women studied, 17% are divorced, compared with only 2.4% of the men. More than half of the executive women who are divorced say their career played a part in the separation.

A study recently completed by James Baron, assistant professor of organizational behavior at Stanford University, and William Bielby, associate professor of sociology at the University of California, Santa Barbara, yields similar results. Using data from the 1960s, the two men studied about 1,000 men and women in a cross section of occupations. Some 86% of their male respondents were married, compared with only 61% of the women.

"As you move up the ladder, these pressures become even greater," Mr. Baron says. "Not only is being married a disadvantage to a woman in that position, but it's an asset for a man."

In 1971, Miss Franklin was appointed to the Nixon White House to recruit women for high-level jobs in the federal government. "Many of them were either single or divorced," she recalls. "It's hard to find men in this age group willing to be supportive and understanding of the demands on a successful woman. I know men who say, 'I support your career. It's wonderful.' But that's not what they mean. They mean I support it as long as it doesn't interfere with someplace I want you to be."

Executive women who are married are generally running the home and bringing home more of the money. On the average these women provide 56% of their household income. Sixty-eight percent of the women say their careers have been more financially rewarding than their husbands', and 78% say their careers have progressed better. About half of the women say they're responsible for the housekeeping, and 29% say they share the work with their spouse. A majority of the women with children say they have the primary responsibility for their care.

"I'm out there writing notes to the housekeeper and arranging meals," says an executive search manager queried about the study. The woman is married to an executive at a large corporation and makes more money than her husband. She says she prefers to do the housework. "I find it easier in life to manage and administer what I've been trained to do," she says, describing how they divide the work at home.

Refusing transfers

Another difference between executive men and women is mobility. While 33% of the female respondents have been asked to relocate, only 21% have done so, compared with 81% of the men. Of the women who refused a transfer, the majority say their refusal hasn't hurt their careers.

While the survey portrays an executive woman who is still bumping into obstacles along the path to success, it also shows her making progress. Nearly half of the women over 52 years of age started in clerical positions, compared with only 23% of the younger female executives, who more often started in management. The younger women also have more earning power than their elders. Some 60% of the women earning more than $106,000 are between 38 and 52, compared with only 20% of those over 52.

Although executive women have more limited educational backgrounds than their male counterparts, more than in the past are graduating from college. Some 20% of the respondents don't have a college degree, compared with 8% of the men surveyed. But 34% of the younger women surveyed have advanced degrees, compared with only 14% of the older women.

Comparison of the two studies shows that female executives are also less conservative and less religious than male executives. Some 60% of the women say religion plays little or no role in their lives, while about the same percentage of men said religion was a significant or moderate influence on them. On economic issues, 49% of the respondents say they are conservative, compared with 74% of the men. On social issues, 21% of the women say they are conservative, compared with 42% of the men. Some 80% of the women favor passage of the Equal Rights Amendment and 90% favor a woman's right to abortion.

The studies also show a difference in family background between men and women in senior management. Sixty percent of the women surveyed say they were either the oldest or only child, compared with 49% of the men. In addition, 48% of the women say they were closer to their fathers while grow-

149

ing up, compared with 40% who were closer to their mothers. Fifty-four percent of these female executives say their mothers didn't work outside the home.

Characteristics of women successful in the male-dominated work world

What, then, can you gather from women's experience in the work world? Here are some tentative conclusions advanced by female advisers:

1. Women can and will have successful careers in the work world despite the male orientation of our society. Women are moving from the "pink collar" jobs (secretaries, assistants, receptionists, etc.) into both service and managerial jobs. The tide is rising and will continue to rise.

2. A woman should expect to meet some prejudice and also to have some advantages in the course of her career. In certain kinds of jobs a woman seems less threatening to the competition than a man; in others she may be at a disadvantage since she cannot enter the Old Boy network and thus through lack of important information and support can be frozen out of certain vital opportunities.

3. A woman who is most likely to get on is one who enjoys her work and remains herself neither denying her femininity nor flaunting it, fitting into the ambience of the organization, believing in its values, developing her professional and managerial skills and showing the same qualities of loyalty and hard work men must show to succeed.

4. Women face an even greater burden than do men of readjusting their marriages and homelife to the demands of their careers and suffer even greater stresses and emotional traumas caused by such conflicts.

5. The percentage of women who are executives and profes-

150

sionals is still relatively small, but the moral sense of our society and the demands of our economy will no longer allow this needless waste of one-half of our human assets through prejudice and discrimination and the denying of opportunity to talent and ambition (see "Is It Worth It?" in Part IV).

Do You Know the Language?

"Jim, we're having an important impromptu meeting. Come if you want to."

"Harry, would you finish that report when you have a chance?"

As in life, so in the work world, people may communicate obliquely. In your organization you must learn how people, particularly executives, express themselves, what kind of language they use, what they mean when they use certain elocutions and indirection.

Are suggestions orders or are they only suggestions?

If Jim is not at the impromptu meeting, he is in serious trouble. If Harry does not finish the report right away and get it in fast, he will find himself on a good-bye list. Both comments are orders, and the mild phrases "if you want to" and "when you have a chance" are simply the way executives express themselves in that company. You must catch on to the way people talk in your organization, learn the language, so to speak, and what it means.

In some organizations, if your boss begins a sentence with "Don't worry, but . . ." you know you should worry. If he offers you a challenge or an opportunity, you know he is going to give you a dirty job nobody else wants or stick you with a no-win situation. If in transferring you to headquarters, the new boss says, "We run a tight ship" or "We're a close-knit staff," it may mean they don't have enough people to do the job and they want you because you're a workaholic. If you find yourself transferred to a group where the boss says, "We're very people-oriented," it may mean, "We don't give raises but we talk nice."

Every organization and each industry has its way of using language and expressing itself—its use of buzz words, circumlocutions and euphemisms. The boss who tells you, "We're very proud of the quality of our operation. We look at what's important," may mean, "We're over budget." As one executive recruiter put it, in the advertising business if they say, "We're a very creative shop," it means the pay is low but you can wear whatever you want to work.

Mary Bralove, summing up the way people talk in a piece in the *Wall Street Journal*, quotes Charles Powell, the movie consultant, on how to respond to a moviemaker after his first screening of a dud. Here are his favorites: "You've done it again, Otto!" "It's all up there on the screen!" "Looks like a million!" "It's nothing but money!" And he says a viewer can imply that he was too moved emotionally to comment on the film by saying, "I really can't talk about it. I'll have to call you tomorrow!"

The language of business can be equally horrifying and more obscure in its euphemisms. One big bank assigns unfortunate rejects to "mobility pools for decruitment." In another large organization you can't just be fired, you have to suffer the indignity of "being impacted by job discontinuance and reassigned for outplacement consultation."

Norman Miller, in an essay, still believes government social scientists remain the unchallenged champions of this kind of language. He points to the use of the terms "unemancipated minors" for teen-agers, "measurable end products" for results, "technology transfer assistance" for giving advice and "effecting linkages" for coordinating.

Learn the buzz words in your organization, but also when your associates and superiors use plain English, learn what they really mean.

Techniques for learning to speak the language

1. Listen (see Listening).

2. Learn the meaning of oblique remarks. When you are not sure of one of these locutions, ask an old-timer: "What is he trying to say to me?"

3. Compile a buzz word list and study it as used in your organization.

4. Keep abreast of the changing fashions in language and words in your field, industry and organization.

Here to conclude our brief lesson in Organization Speak, let us offer The Manager's Dictionary for those who wish to understand executive talk, and for those who do research a Researcher's Dictionary:

EXECUSPEAK

A program—Any assignment that can't be completed by one telephone call

Program implementation—Hiring more people

An expeditor—a person who confounds confusion with a commotion

A coordinator—the guy whose desk is between two expeditors

A reliable source—The guy you just met

An informed source—The one who told the guy you just met

A zealot—One who redoubles his efforts as he loses sight of his goals

Reorientation—Getting used to working again

Under consideration—Never heard of it

Under active consideration—We're looking for it in the files

Please note and initial—Let's spread the responsibility for this

And for the Researcher:

"It has long been known . . ." I haven't bothered to look it up

"Of great theoretical and practical importance . . ." Of interest to me

"It is believed that . . ." I think

"It is generally believed that . . ." Someone else thinks so too

"It is clear that much additional work will be required before a complete understanding . . ." I don't understand it

"Correct within some order of magnitude . . ." Wrong

"It is to be hoped that this work will stimulate further research in this field . . ." We didn't do anything with this subject but then nor did anyone else

"Thanks are due John Doe for assistance with this research and to Jack Smith for valuable discussions . . ." Doe did the work and Smith explained what it meant to me

"I'm Running This"

If any project is to get done, someone has to run it. If it is yours, take charge.

How do you take charge?

You get advice. You plan. You set a deadline.

Second, you organize.

If others are involved, you try to get them together and outline your plan, get their agreement on the plan and on the deadline. If you can't get them together, go to each, one by one, and do the above. Always get agreement from each person on his or her deadline for his or her part in the project.

Third, you administer.

You keep on top of the plan. You do your part. You offer

help if you see one of the others needs it or is in trouble with his or her agreed-upon contribution.

You cheer everybody along. Your project may not be particularly important to the others, since it may not be their main job, so you must make it as easy and pleasant for them as possible.

Fourth, you control.

If someone is falling behind, you help bring him along to agreed-upon standards. If the contributions are not adequate, you help make them so. You see that the job is being done right and that the deadline will be met.

You take charge of any project given you. You see that it is completed—on time, on target.

Temperament

Can you afford temperament?

The answer is sometimes.

You are not a zombie, and within reason you should express your feelings and opinions—within reason. There are five kinds of temperament, however, you cannot afford:

You cannot afford temper tantrums in front of anybody.

You cannot afford strongly delivered opinions on religion or politics, unless you are a minister or politician.

You cannot afford any sort of physical altercation.

You cannot afford remarks that wound people in their most sensitive areas.

You cannot afford revealing deep-seated prejudices against people by reason of race, creed, color or sex.

Almost all of us have strong or deep feelings about something. Almost all of us have prejudices that, though perhaps subconscious, are nevertheless deeply felt. Almost all of us have periods when we want to explode in violence of some sort.

155

Temper tantrums

Certain executives have found anger and the temper tantrum a good way of getting things done under certain circumstances. They use anger and explosion to manage. This is a very dangerous method. It may be effective sometimes but it also cuts the user off from relationships that could fulfill his career and his life and builds enmity that may destroy him.

The temper tantrum you may have simply as a response to what you consider intolerable provocation is also dangerous. As an adult you must have worked out some way to relieve your feelings that protects you from such explosions in the office or around people or at home: the workout in a gym, jogging, some physical activity that will drain off the anger or at least channel it away from an explosion in public. You cannot afford temper tantrums.

Opinions on religion or politics

You must leave your soapbox at home.

You have a right to your opinions and beliefs and you may hold them strongly but you cannot afford to deliver them on the job with unbecoming vehemence unless that is your job. If you are in politics, your political opinions are relevant. If you are a minister or rabbi, your religious views are relevant. Otherwise, in the work world, they are private and almost never relevant to your job. Keep them to yourself.

Physical altercations

This is insane. Unless in self-defense, you completely sever any relationship you may have in the work world.

Wounding people in particularly sensitive areas

Bill Keeler is fat. He was a fat boy. He is a fat man. And he hates it. You joke with him. You call him Fatso. He smiles or

156

laughs. He knows you are joking but he will hate you nevertheless. You have wounded him in a particularly sensitive area. It is irrational but there it is. Learn where people are sensitive and do not gore them in that area.

Prejudices

Your prejudices, or if you prefer to call them aversions, to blacks, Italians, Jews, women or Lithuanians do not belong in public. Nor will the phrase "some of my best friends are Lithuanians" excuse such a prejudice. You may not be able to help your dislike of classes of peoples; you may even have good reason to hate certain classes or nationalities. There was the Armenian genocide in Turkey. There was the Holocaust. But in the workplace, the revelations of your hatreds may hurt many innocent people. Furthermore, certain prejudices, if they injure innocent people through discrimination, are actionable. Keep such prejudices out of the work world.

Once again, you are not a zombie. You have feelings and you should be able to express them within reason. Learn what displays of temperament you cannot afford and avoid them.

What Does He Really Want?

One of the hard lessons you will learn in the work world is that people do not always want what they say they want. And sometimes if you do give them what they say they want, they won't like it.

> "You know, Tim, I don't like all this hoopla about the honor I got. Let's play it down a bit. I feel we all did it. The honor belongs to a lot of others who helped me too. It would embarrass me to take all the credit."
>
> This is the old man, the president, speaking, and Tim is the editor of the company paper. He also puts out the releases. Privately he also agrees with the old

man that the honor came to him because of the company. So he plays it down.

The old man calls him in.

"I'm a little disappointed, Tim, in the story you did on the governor's award to me. It didn't have the zing you usually put into our publication, and I notice we didn't get any pickup at all on the release."

"But, Mr. Bryant, you asked me to play it down, not to make too much of it."

"It was all wasted, Tim" the old man says sadly, "all wasted."

Later Lillian Simmons, the public relations vice-president, calls him in.

"For heaven's sake, Tim," she says, "don't you know the old man loves publicity whatever he says? You didn't even send along his picture. Am I going to have to look at everything you do?"

"But he expressly told me to play it down, Lillian," Tim repeats. "He was very emphatic about it."

"Tim," Lillian says tiredly, "haven't you learned to figure out what people mean and not pay too much attention to what they say? The old man pulls the "little old me" routine all the time, but he loves the limelight. Besides, he deserved that award."

Now let us look at another version of the same thing.

The president is studying the new company letterhead. His executive vice-president is sitting across from him.

"You know, Ed," he says, holding up the letter paper, don't you think putting our logo on the company letterhead is sort of tacky?"

"I'll take care of it, PJ," the executive vice-president says.

Suddenly the logo is gone—not just from the letterhead but from everything—all publications, the plant entrances, headquarters, the lot.

"What happened?" the president asks.

"Our ad agency is getting us a new logo," the executive vice-president says. "I told them you thought this logo looked tacky. I ordered them taken down."

"My God, Clem," the president exclaims, "I didn't say I thought the logo looked tacky. I think it's great. I just said I thought putting it on our letterhead was a bit tacky."

"Oh," the executive vice-president says.

What does he really mean?

There is a saying among linguists, "Words don't mean anything; people mean something."

Techniques for understanding what is really wanted

1. Listen (see "Listening").
2. Know to whom you are talking or find out about the person.
3. Understand what the person is really saying, not necessarily what seems to be said. Ask someone who knows the person to help you interpret what he or she is looking for.
4. Use your own judgment. You are paid to do a job, not just to carry out orders. Stand up for what is good, within your competence.
5. Listen.

Power

As you go up in your career, you will acquire power and influence in the organization, and the puzzling question may arise as to how this power came to you, how it can be preserved and how it should be used.

Power is not just office politics. Despite the folklore, it generally is not achieved through skulduggery or underhanded means. And often it is widely misunderstood. Many do not even recognize power when they see it. Power may be defined as the possession of control, authority or influence over others, and it arises from three principal sources: position, personality and contribution.

You may have quickly recognized who are the powerful people in your organization and in some cases wondered why or how they achieved their power. In other cases you may have not understood how powerful certain people were and have underestimated them, to your career's detriment. You yourself may not realize where your power lies or where and when it can be used. Power is not something a person owns: it is what others give to him or her. It is usually earned over a period of time but, like fame, it can evaporate in a day or so. Here are the most common sources of power in an organization:

Position

Your most obvious source of power is the title and position you have earned in the company. In viable organizations the position assigned you gives you certain prerogatives. It gives you authority as well as responsibility. It delineates, usually through organization charts, who reports to you and where you stand in the hierarchy. The power given by the position, however, obvious as it is, is usually not sufficient to enable the jobholder to wield the kind of power necessary to advance his career fully in the organization. And sometimes the title is deceptive. It may conceal the fact that the person has reached a plateau or has been assigned an empty position without power.

On the other hand, a person may land a powerful position

but then forfeit it through nonuse or misuse of that power, perhaps by delegating functions that should be attended to personally, such as budgeting or purchasing, where the allocation of resources are involved. Or the person may raise enemies among opinion leaders or alienate those reporting to him or her, thus destroying the power base. It must always be remembered that power comes from without, not from within. It is always given by others or allowed by the acquiescence of others, and it can be withdrawn or sabotaged, no matter how legitimate, if it is not used, or if it is misused or undermined by others.

Personality

The second source of power in an organization is personality—the ability to win friends and influence people. There are people whose superior ability, attractiveness, sensitivity and warmth make them opinion or taste leaders in any organization no matter what position they occupy (see "Opinion Leaders"). They are natural leaders, and others are influenced by their opinions and ideas. They are often the center of a network of persons who admire them or are influenced by them and who themselves hold key positions. Thus, a word from an opinion leader can sometimes move mountains of resistance and get a project through.

Contribution

The third source of power arises through the contribution you make to the success or profitability of the enterprise or of individuals in the enterprise. The more important your contribution, the greater your power, and an organization will go to great lengths to satisfy someone whose skill is essential to its survival.

There are others whose length of service has stored up a reservoir of accomplishments that give these veterans power in certain areas, and finally there is the power you have stored up through helping others, through the favors you have done—personal contributions where you can imply with a smile, "Now you owe me one." Favors, of course, are a major source of political power, and as you rise in any organization, you will have more and more opportunities to store up this kind of power.

Techniques, tactics and strategies to use in gaining and conserving power

1. Use all the authority given you by your position. Authority that is not used may be withdrawn. Do not, however, misuse it or use it in such a way that you alienate those affected by it.

2. Power lies in friendships and relationships. Cultivate your ability to relate to people, to form friendships and warm ties. Become part of a network, if you can.

3. Know who the opinion and taste leaders are in your organization and in your field and insofar as possible become acquainted with them. If these people are behind you, most of your projects will go through.

4. Cultivate an attitude and habit of doing others favors when you can. Make others look good. They will not forget it and will be a reservoir of support when you need it.

5. Do good work and be loyal and you will accumulate power in any organization.

New Position

One of the most difficult adjustments you will make is that of a promotion to a managerial position from a job where you are "one of the gang." When you become a manager, your view of the world and your relationship with your associates must change.

It is not simply that some of your former associates may resent your promotion for a variety of reasons—envy, a sense that it should have been they rather than you, or dismay at someone else's good fortune—it is that they know you, your strengths and your weaknesses, and having known you as a friend and an associate, they may have difficulty in adjusting to your status as a manager.

But you must accept certain realities that this new position imposes on you. You are no longer an associate, you are a manager, and in the words of John J. McCarthy in his book *Why Managers Fail* "you must be willing to pay the price of being a manager, i.e., being lonely."

Nor is it that you have suddenly become snobbish and think you are too good for your old associates. It is the nature of the new position. You must now leave behind two major relationships—your attachment to your old job function and your warm relationship as "one of the gang"—if you expect to fulfill your role as a manager. You must step back and look at your old function and job with eyes of a manager as just one of the jobs to be managed and your old associates in a more aloof and businesslike fashion, if you wish them to respect you and your new position.

There are traumatic aspects of this new position. You may sometimes leave behind friendships. You will have a tendency to miss the function you have left behind and sometimes to try to cling to it. Peter Drucker has said that a manager in assigning work should always assign some function to himself besides the work of managing, and while this may be true and perhaps you should, as they say, keep your hand in, you must not cling to your old function in such a way that your main role as a manager is affected.

Your second trauma is that the new position, if properly filled, will affect your friendships with your former associates.

In *Why Managers Fail* John J. McCarthy explains this form of managerial difficulty as follows:

> The genesis of this managerial failure is the desire of too many managers to be *liked* instead of striving to be *respected!* Intensive research among a group of 900 successful managers indicated that as they analyzed the earlier years of their careers, when they were in nonmanagerial positions, the managers they had found to be most effective were categorized as "fair but firm." Significantly, few of their earlier bosses whom they regarded as "nice" were listed as having been particularly helpful in the development of their subordinates, or as having contributed significantly to the later success of those subordinates.
>
> The foregoing is not an endorsement of the maxim "nice guys don't win ball games." It is certainly not meant to imply that a successful manager must be cold and distant. It *is* meant to imply that successful managers develop an ability to maintain balance. . . . [They] will know where to draw the line between familiarity and "unapproachability" without being regarded as curt, distant, or lacking in interest in employees as people.

These areas, then, are psychologically the most difficult of the adjustments you will have to make as a manager. The compensations are many: increased status, increased salary, more opportunity to make a difference and contribution in the company, more power and, not least, a broader view, a wider horizon, higher ground from which to view the world. You will, of course, have to live up to this increased potential. You will have to take some form of continuing education. You will have to look at the organization more carefully, take more responsibility for its welfare and learn a great deal more about it. You will have to increase your ability to communicate and to get along with others on all levels. You will have to sharpen your social skills and learn more about human nature.

Moving to a new position in the management world is a major leap. Of all the things you must learn, these are the ones that you must learn fastest if you are to succeed:

**Tactics and strategies in moving to a new
managerial position**

1. Learn the function of managing (see *Who Depends on Me?*)

2. Learn to leave behind your present function or, if you take some of it with you, to place it in its proper frame of reference as just another job, no more or less important than the other jobs you must manage.

3. Learn to change, if necessary gradually, the relationships you have with your old associates so that you gain their respect and they will regard you as a manager and give your new position the authority it deserves.

4. Learn to regard the company from a broader perspective, to become more aware of the whole enterprise with respect to its operations, its goals, its policies and the management relationships generally.

5. If you have not already done so, sit down and plan your career, where you want to be one year, five years, ten years from now. If you have already done this, you need to look at this new position and see how it fits into that overall plan (see "Career").

Career

Jobholders who succeed best map their careers. They do not leave everything to chance. They look at their careers—one of the two most important elements of their lives, the love relationship being the other—with a manager's eye and they try to plan their career so that it will fulfill their capacities, their needs and their dreams.

Goethe is reputed to have said something to this effect: "Beware of what you desire in your youth for you will get it in middle age," and Delmore Schwartz used the title "In Dreams Begin Responsibilities."

Some techniques, tactics and strategies in mapping a career

The first step is a careful self-analysis. It should deal with four major questions:

—What are your dreams? Where do you want to see yourself at the height of your career?

—What are your strengths, your assets, both in the job and out of it?

—What are your weaknesses? What kinds of work do you fail in or wish to avoid? What areas do you need to strengthen yourself in? What areas of knowledge or self-cultivation must you pursue?

—What kind of life-style do you wish to achieve? City, suburb, metropolitan center? Travel? What range of income and what kinds of assets?

John J. McCarthy, a career management consultant, produced a career management plan that asks 117 very specific questions. They generally fit into and supplement the major questions above. These major questions you may have only vaguely contemplated. They may still not be completely answerable. You may not have reached this degree of self-knowledge, but at least they should be asked and pondered.

Your second step requires setting down on paper those goals you have been able to identify and set at least on a tentative basis, and it requires attempting to quantify and make them as concrete as possible.

1. Write out your short-range goals on the job: what you want to accomplish this year and the next.

2. Second, write out as best you can your long-range goals: five or ten years or more ahead.

3. Third, consider your life-style and the way your family would like to live and how the goals you have set can help bring about that life-style.

4. Finally, map out the things you will have to do to reach these goals, those moves in your power, the courses you must take, your personal reading program, the allocation of your time and effort and how everything can be worked out in relation to your obligations to your family and others.

The main thing about dreams is not that we have them but that we do not dream deeply or richly enough. Our goals are set too low, our dreams too small. Dream to your capacities. Build a career you can be proud of that uses all your abilities and interests and desires. For the fact is that deeply desired dreams, deeply worked-out dreams, tend to come true.

SELF-ASSESSMENT ON PART III, "RELATIONSHIPS"

Your job depends more on your ability to maintain relationships with your associates and your supervisor and with the values, principles, culture and aspirations of the organization itself that on any other aspect of your work. This self-assessment will address situations arising from these relationships and how you can handle them. Relevant discussions are indicated in suggested answers and references to these self-assessments on pages 270–279.

1. How would you describe your relationship with your boss?

2. How would you describe your boss's standing in the organization and relationship with his or her superiors?

3. What would you do if you found that:

- You went into a meeting with the wrong information and realized certain key new information had deliberately not been sent to you, although all the others at the meeting had received it?

- You went to a superior with a new idea and he said, "We tried that some years ago, and it didn't work." Subsequently the idea is put into effect by this man in precisely the words you presented it in your memorandum but credited to this superior?

- You find you have been subtly criticized by a rival in front of your boss and associated with a disastrous project with which you had nothing to do?

- You are put in charge of a project that depends on the cooperation of members of a bureaucracy and find that you are the victim of malicious obedience, imbecilic goodwill and selective amnesia and cannot get anything through?

- You are told by a "kind friend" that someone is out to get you and that so-and-so does not like you?

4. If you need to get something done fast, what is usually the best communication channel to reach the person or persons who can do it?

5. How would you describe the way people in your organization deal with those reporting to them and with their superiors?

6. What are the key characteristics that could make you a good listener?

7. What would you do if you were asked to speak frankly to your superior about an important shortcoming? If you were asked to speak frankly to someone who reported to you?

8. You dislike an associate. You hear a bad rumor about this person. Should you pass it on, since you know it is true and it would forewarn others?

9. Do your job relationships suffer because you tend to be a loner, and what do you do about it?

10. You are disheartened by the constant waste caused by a deeply entrenched and inefficient procedure in your division's operations. You write a strong memorandum showing the magnitude of the waste and the stupidity of the procedure. Should you send it?

11. You are asked to make a presentation persuading management to make a drastic change. What are your first considerations when preparing the presentation?

12. You have landed in a job with a constantly complaining, arrogant, credit-grabbing, unreasonable boss. What do you do?

13. You are astounded to be told by a friend that someone on the job dislikes you. What possible reason could he have?

14. You find a rival associate has damaged your reputation through innuendo and rumor. What can you do about it?

15. You need someone to help you along in the organization. How do you go about finding such a person?

16. No one seems to tell you anything. You seem to be missing the rumors and the gossip and you wonder vaguely why you are to be left out of it all. What can you do to plug into the grapevine?

17. You find your boss difficult to understand, half the time seeming to say things he or she really does not mean. What should you do?

18. What people in the organization should you make an effort to get to know?

19. You find your loyalty is questioned because you have expressed disagreement with several company policies. How can you gauge whether you are loyal or not?

20. You find yourself in a group that seems to have very low morale. What can you do?

21. You are an attractive woman and suddenly you realize your boss is suggesting that you have dinner with him if you wish to progress in your career. How is it best to handle this?

22. You and a divorced associate have drifted into an affair. Can your job be endangered by this relationship?

23. What are the most common obstacles a woman faces as she rises in the business world?

24. You are given an assignment without any formal authority to carry it out. What do you do?

25. You have a moment of blowing off steam in front of the wrong people. Is your career ruined?

26. Your boss tells you not to bother about her in making arrangements for a ceremony—she doesn't mind where you put her. She doesn't want any special consideration. What does she mean?

27. You are very anxious to put over a cherished project. What sources of power are available to you in getting it accepted?

28. You have been promoted to head the group. You overhear one of the old gang saying, "I guess the promotion went to Roger's head. He wasn't at the Friday-night gripe session and beer bust." Should you have gone?

29. It is midnight and you have been thinking about your job and your life. You wonder whether you are going the right way. What should you do?

PART IV

□

THE OUTSIDE WORK WORLD
—TWENTY-NINE Things You Should Know about whether You Have the Right Job and Are Being Paid Enough

Do you know your worth in the marketplace?

Do you know what the demand for your kind of job is? Do you even know whether you are in the right job for your abilities and proclivities?

These are some of the things you can find out by taking a foray from time to time into the outside world to see what is going on, what the demands are, who the people are, what kind of work is being done. We are not suggesting jobhopping just to get a little more money or changing a possible career because the job you have is not perfect for you. Leaving a job for any reason is a serious move. You leave not just the work and the money, not even just the benefits, though this is a serious consideration. You also leave relationships and a reputation that you have built up over the years and that must be rebuilt in any new job.

Looking Around

Bob Hall ran into a former classmate.

"So you're with Electronics, Inc.," the classmate said after their preliminary handshake and update, when they found they were with similar organizations. "I suppose you're going to be at the follow-up conference on the Dwyer circuitry."

"The follow-up conference?" Bob asked.

"Weren't you at the society's annual meeting in October, Bob?" the classmate asked. "They discussed a new approach on the kind of circuitry for some of these components, and they think Banlon's new microprocessors may be the wave of the future."

When they parted after agreeing to get together again, Bob was thoughtful. He had read the paper on the new circuitry and discussed it with the others in his group at his firm, but he realized he had missed a lot of the outside discussion on it by engineers from other companies. He also realized he had become so immersed in the problems of his job that he had no idea what was going on in some important areas of his profession.

All our advisers emphasized that it was important to keep a window open on the world. No matter how happy you are in your job or how absorbing it is, there are major benefits in knowing what is going on in the outside world—benefits to you and benefits to the organization.

The benefits to you are obvious. You may outgrow the job, or it may outgrow you. The organization may change or may experience hard times and your prospects diminish. Or you may not be receiving adequate salary or benefits as compared with others in your kind of job. Or you may feel the need to move into another area.

The benefits to the organization are not so clear, but the jobholder who keeps open his contacts and keeps his eye on the outside world will bring into the company advances in his work and help keep his organization abreast of new developments. Though this is not recognized, our economy in large organizations provides a form of lifetime employment to most people, if they want it. The breadth and complexity of the work in most large organizations usually provide challenges enough for most careers, and the social ambience of the organization engenders a strong bond of loyalty and social values that enrich the jobholder's life but may close him in from contact with the outside world.

Questions to ask in assessing your position in relation to the outside world

Even though you are satisfied with your work and your organization and fulfilled in the work life you are leading within that organization, ask yourself these questions:

1. Do I know what is going on in my field of interest and expertise outside of my own organization?
2. Do I know others in my field in other organizations who might be helpful in expanding my knowledge and understanding of my work?
3. Have I built up a network of outside contacts of friends or business acquaintances to whom I can turn for advice or counsel or simply to exchange information and experience beneficial to me and my organization?

If the answers are no, you would do well to open these windows on the world.

Sizing Up the Market

The market—like the moon on the tides—exerts a heavy pull on the economy and thus on the personnel needs of organizations.

Skills, experience and competence in four major areas are necessary to the operations and survival of any organization. The areas are:

Research and development
Engineering and production
Marketing
Accounting and finance

Your contribution to the organization will usually fall into one of these broad areas, and in the restless ocean of the economy, at certain times skills, experience and competence in one of these areas will become more valuable or necessary to the survival of the organization than those in any of the other broad areas. During these periods the needed background, experience and competence will command higher salaries and more prestige, though this will vary according to the organization.

You can often tell by the background of the chief executive and high officers where the organization places its greatest prestige. At one time in many organizations, engineering was king and the chief executive came from a background of engineering or production. Then mass marketing needs brought marketing to the top, particularly in consumer industries, and the chief executive usually had a marketing background (or advertising or sales or some other marketing aspect), and marketing was king. When hard times came, finance and accounting became king. Then in certain high-technology companies, research and development became king to help solve urgent technological problems and develop new products, and the chief executive had a technical and scientific background or was an inventor/developer type. So the needs of different organizations in the fluctuating economy brought different skills, experience and background to the privileged positions in the organization and the economy.

As a jobholder you will notice the fluctuating demand for your kind of skill and experience. You will notice it within the organization, but you should also notice it in the outside world. You may be in an organization that values another area of skill and experience, say engineering and production, while it seems to downgrade yours, say marketing, when in the outside world your area has become a premium asset. In such a case you may need to consider whether your career would not be better served in another organization, even though you have built up a reputation and a circle of friends and found a home in your own organization. The latter circumstances may, however, outweigh the downgrading of your area, and of course your area could gain in prestige as the needs of your organization change. Regardless, it is important from time to time to size up the market for your kind of skills, experience and background in the outside world.

Techniques and tactics in assessing the market for your skill and experience

1. Keep abreast of what is going on in the economy by reading business magazines and papers. Business news has become very important, and even general daily papers carry news of business.

2. Note the demand for certain backgrounds by company university recruiters and the relative starting salaries for graduates with these backgrounds and degrees. Engineering degrees were always desirable but fell in value at one period when an oversupply of engineering graduates came on the market. Today they are once again in fashion. The same happened in other areas. The graduate business degree, the MBA, has become extremely popular in recent years and, when received from prestige schools, commands high starting salaries. Twenty years ago business degrees had little standing.

3. Talk to your network of outside friends in business and find out the standing of your kind of background in their companies.

It is useful and important, if you cherish your work and your career, to step out and look at the market for people with your background, experience and skills from time to time. This will help you assess your worth in the marketplace.

Are You Being Paid What You're Worth?

Except in the most unusual or esoteric jobs or in cases of exceptional gifts, it is not difficult to find out whether you are being paid what you're worth.

Organizations have two ways of valuing a job: the going rate, that is, the value the present market has placed on the job, and the internal policy and cost structure of the organization itself. Large organizations usually have a wage and salary program that includes job specifications with grouping and ranking of jobs, a compensation structure that is the result of market surveys and the posture the company wants to have in these various job markets.

You can usually find out the salary range for your kind of job, particularly if your work has been given a job specification. If you have built an outside network, you can also find out roughly the salaries of people in your kind of job in the marketplace. You cannot ordinarily find out salaries of your associates in the company on an individual basis. Few wish to share that information, although rumor and gossip may supply moderately accurate estimates.

A person's salary is an especially sensitive area since it may also be the value the organization places on him as a person. If you are in the lower range or below the range of salaries for your kind of job, you must wonder whether you and your capabilities are highly thought of in the company. Organizations usually take into account the length of time you have been with them and if you have been with the organization over a year without a raise, since inflation tends to decrease your salary's buying power, you must consider whether you came in at a rate that has hit the ceiling for that job or whether your work has been less than satisfactory or whether the company is experiencing hard times.

Ordinary compensation in our society generally includes benefits—health and accident insurance, vacations and pensions—and these often equal as much as 30 to 40 percent of the total compensation package. They have become particularly valuable since your pension may be fully vested after a certain number of years with the organization and you may carry it with you if you move to another organization. It is important to know what benefits an organization offers and take them into account in considering your compensation (see "Benefits").

While most jobs are offered without contracts or agreements as to duration, organizations may offer employment contracts for top management positions, usually for one to five years and renewable. These contracts may specify benefits, bonuses, stock options and deferred compensation arrangements, all of which are negotiated. These offers are usually for only the highest positions or for exceptional skills, either professional or scientific.

Most of us come in on an indefinite basis without a contract and without support by a union. We may leave when we wish but we may also be discharged by the organization "at will," that is, for any or no reason with very few exceptions (see Part V). Most organizations value jobholders highly and set the compensation structure to hold their best people indefinitely throughout a career. Nevertheless, you must consider whether you are being paid what you're worth in the marketplace.

Techniques for learning whether you are being paid what you are worth

1. Keep in touch with economic trends by reading business magazines and newspapers.

2. Find out the organization's compensation structure and the range of pay for your type of job by consulting the personnel department or your boss.

3. Ask around outside for information as to what is being

179

paid for your kind of work and experience and what the demand is for people with your background.

4. Ask people in an employment agency or an executive recruiter what the going rates are for someone with your experience and skills.

Jumping

Leaving a job for any reason is a serious move, but there are situations where this may be in your best interests. Jumping from one job to another and over short periods of time, however, is rarely in your interest and may be a symptom of some underlying psychological difficulty.

When prospective employers or executive recruiters look at a background sheet or résumé where the applicant has been with four or five different organizations in as many years, this naturally raises a question as to the candidate's reliability as a jobholder. The ability to impress people and good connections may give you access to a number of jobs in succession, but if you keep leaving the work after the initial pleasure of something new wears off or if you are found to be unsatisfactory for whatever reason, you must sit down and consider what it is about you—your personality, your priorities, your life-style—that makes it difficult for you to stay in one job for any length of time.

Psychologists suggest several possibilities:

—A restlessness that is not suited to organizational life but may be suited to a profession that presents a variety of client problems or to an entrepreneurial enterprise that requires you to do all things at all times.

—An ego problem that makes you unable to endure a situation where you are not constantly the center of attention and thus causes you to jump to something else as soon as the job becomes routine and the focus of attention turns away from you.

—An inability to handle the detail and scutwork that any job entails.

—An ambition that will not permit you to remain on a job you feel beneath your abilities.

—A fear of being found to be less able than you have presented yourself as being or of having pretensions revealed that seem necessary to your self-esteem.

—An unfortunate selection of organizations that failed or went out of business or were merged.

Four steps to consider in remedying the job-hopping syndrome

1. Sit down and identify the reasons you either left each of your short-term four or five jobs or were discharged from them. Try to be honest and objective about the situation, painful though that may be.

2. If the reasons reveal that you do not belong in an organizational environment, consider whether you can reorient your background to enter the academic or entrepreneurial worlds and what steps you must take to enter these different job worlds.

3. If the reasons seem to have the psychological aspects indicated as ego or ambition problems or self-esteem difficulties, you may need help. You might discuss the matter with your spouse or a trusted friend.

4. Select your next job carefully and stick to it long enough to put down roots and gain the experience, capability, self-confidence and expertise that a good job gives.

Sitting Still

And yet, you can stay too long in one job.

Ted Clifton turned to his friend, Joe, and said bitterly, "Look at Jeff Coles. They've transferred him to

181

the Quality Keys group. I've been here twice as long as he and I do twice as good a job and they've never offered me a chance like that.''

"But, Ted, it isn't a promotion," Joe said. "It's just a transfer. And besides, why would they want to transfer you—you're one of our best people. Jeff's a slob. They wanted to get rid of him. They 'sold' him to the Quality Key people—wait til QK sees what it got.''

Ted was silent a moment.

"Well," he said, "that makes me feel a little better, but I wanted to go to QK—it's a hot operation. What do I have to do to get out of here—lousy work?''

Good workers sometimes stay too long in one job and for a number of reasons:

—Like Ted Clifton, they may be so good at their job that the manager does not want to let them go. Bad managers hoard good workers, thus depriving them of development and opportunity.

—They may, like another member of a group, Tim Ellsworth, be so comfortable in the job they do not want to move. This is not the same as reaching your capacity level or going as far as you can with your abilities. It is a form of laziness and it usually results in lack of development and opportunity. Tim will get bored with the job and eventually want to go on but he will find that he has not prepared himself or made the proper moves and has been left behind.

—They may not have looked around and become aware of what the organization has to offer.

—They may have become stymied in that organization and, because of family obligations, not have had the chance to look around outside for something better.

—They may not be willing to take any kind of risk for their

182

career. You cannot have a true career without taking some risks.

Jumping, as we have discussed, is not good, but neither is sitting still beyond a certain point. A job is a big part of your life. When you have mastered it or when you have plumbed its possibilities, it is time to look around. Here are some questions to ask yourself if you find yourself sitting still too long:

Steps to consider if you feel you have stayed in one job too long

1. Have you worked out a career path for yourself (see Part III, "Career")?

2. Do you know what possibilities and opportunities are open to you? If there are no better jobs than the one you have in that group, are there in other groups in the company?

3. Have you made any outside contacts with friends or former classmates in the work world and can you learn from them what opportunities exist in your area in other organizations?

4. Have you talked with your boss about your career desires and about possibilities for advancement or opportunities to broaden your job experience?

Stay in the job long enough to pay your dues to it, to get from it the experience and mastery you need and to show your mettle. But do not sit still forever. You owe the company reasonable competence, reliability and longevity in your job. You owe yourself a career.

People in My Job

One of the great advantages your contacts in the outside world give you is knowing others who work in the same kind of job as yours or in the same profession or area of work.

To make these contacts, you need to find out what organizations, societies or professional bodies there are in your field. You need to join them, if your credentials permit, and go to their meetings or conferences. If you are an engneer, you should join one of the engineering societies, if an accountant, one of the accounting bodies, if in marketing, some marketing association, if in business communications, public affairs or the like, one of the societies such as the International Association of Business Communicators or the Public Relations Society. If none of these, perhaps one of the management associations such as the Conference Board or the American Management Association.

At meetings of the society in your field or in courses given by management associations, you will get to know people who have your kind of job and you will be able to compare notes and problems and make valuable friendships. Most organizations welcome your joining such societies, and some will pay for your membership or your courses, since it is to the organization's advantage for you to know what is going on in your field.

Whether your organization will support you or not in this, you should keep this window on the world open for your own sake. Secondly, you should develop personal friendships with others in jobs similar to yours in other organizations. These friendships are enriching in themselves, since you and people in your kind of work have so much in common. Further, such friendships often lead to opportunities in the work world and in other organizations.

Finally, you may get to know people in your field who may have similar jobs but with a different orientation than the one you have. If yours is a staff job, a support service to direct economic production in your organization, and you know someone with a similar line job, one that is directly productive to the organization's main product or service, you can learn how your friend operates in that capacity as against how you must operate in your staff capacity.

All these approaches to those in jobs similar to your own will give you knowledge and insight into your own job and into its possibilities in the outside world.

Here are four recommended approaches:

Strategies and tactics to expand your skills and qualifications in your job through outside contacts

1. Join a society or group dedicated to your field.

2. Go to the meetings and make friends with those in other organizations who have your kind of job.

3. If possible, become active in the society or association. This is often time-consuming and sometimes expensive but it has many rewards.

4. Keep in contact with people in your kind of job in other organizations and have lunch with one or another of them from time to time to talk over mutual job interests.

Moonlighting

Moonlighting means working at another job outside of the primary job for which you were hired.

"Tim," Joe Hanley said, "I understand you do some consulting on the side."

"True, Joe."

"It's the same kind of work you're doing for us, isn't it?"

"Well, not exactly, Joe."

"It has to do with engineering like that on the Keystone Project, doesn't it?"

"Well, to some degree, but Chacona isn't in competition with us, Joe. They're just a little company getting started, and I'm only doing this on the side, evenings and weekends.''

"Tim," Joe said, "you either want to work for us or for them. You can't do both. There's a conflict of interest there. Even if they're small, they're in competition with us, and we can't keep you if you have this other job on the side."

"All right, Joe . . ."

Joe Henley is right in this case, and Tim is violating the policy of most organizations that hire on a full-time basis and expect the services for which they have hired you to be exclusively for them.

Now let us look at another situation.

Harry Brett works at Calman's as a salesclerk during the day. At five o'clock, after a day's work, he has dinner and then, to supplement his income, he spends two hours three times a week tutoring the two sons of Dr. Kinney in mathematics.

There can be no conflict of interest in his moonlighting in this way, and as long as he discharges his duties as a salesclerk adequately, the store should have no interest in, or objection to, his other job.

Just as you can have other outside activities, volunteer work and the like, so one of these outside activities can be a second job if it does not conflict with or make you less able to perform the work you have been hired to do for the primary organization. However, it must be work that does not bring on a conflict of interest with your primary job and it must not be so demanding that you cannot give your primary job the hours and effort it requires.

It often happens that you may need to take on extra work, another job to make ends meet, to broaden your abilities, to increase your independence, to move into a new area or for other reasons. In the old days employers did not take kindly to moonlighting. Many organizations still do not. They want all of your paid efforts, but times have changed, and if you take on another job or if from time to time you moonlight, here are five things to consider:

1. Check company policy to see whether any restrictions apply to doing outside work for pay and what these restrictions are. If there is nothing in writing on this, ask your supervisor or personnel what the policy is.

2. Be sure the job you wish to moonlight on is not for the same services you are performing for the primary company or, if it is, be sure there is no conflict of interest or competitive factor involved between the primary organization and your operations for the other employer.

3. If policy in your primary organization is too restrictive in this area, go to your boss or some appropriate authority and try to get a special dispensation. Be aware, however, that in some cases the knowledge that you are moonlighting may affect your career with the primary company. It is possible those responsible for your promotions may feel you are not committed enough to the main organization and its work.

4. If you are discouraged from such outside work or if it seems that your opportunities in the primary organization will be limited by such outside work but you still want the other job for whatever reason, consider whether your services to your primary organization can be converted into a consulting arrangement that could permit you to provide them to the other job also. Such an arrangement, however, will generally lose you the valuable benefits that full-scale employment offers, in particular pension benefits. A consulting arrangement may have advantages for the primary company in eliminating these rather expensive fringe benefits, but that organization may wish to restrict the job to a full-time employee.

5. If the primary organization is adamant, you must make a

187

choice. You may work out an arrangement with the second employer that permits you to work for others. You must assess carefully what is in your best interests both financially and psychologically, what will give you both emotional security and a rewarding career. If you decide in favor of your primary employer, you must play fair and work only for the primary employer, on its terms.

Your Résumé

In the end, whether you leave or stay, you should make up a background sheet on yourself, a résumé.

The résumé is a sort of calling card. It gives your name and address and telephone numbers for home and business. It lists the jobs you have had, usually from the present backward to the first, your educational background, your professional or community associations and honors, your interests. While you are not required to give your age or marital status or other kinds of information regarding matters that might be construed as militating against you because of age, sex, color, et cetera, the more information you provide in the résumé, the more likely you will be to attract the kind of employer you seek. The résumé will usually not get you the job but it may get you the interview you want.

Résumés, of course, vary, but here is a list of the items that most personnel directors and executive recruiters say they look for and that employers are usually impressed by. Following this is a list of those characteristics of a résumé that usually raise a question in the minds of personnel directors, employers and others.

Items that are usually looked for in a résumé

1. The kind of job or area you are most interested in, what you are applying for generally.

188

2. Your work record, companies you have worked for and jobs you have had, with dates, beginning with your present or last job and going backward to the first.

3. Business accomplishments in these jobs and for these companies (example: "Negotiated a reduction of bank's compensating balance for company that freed up $2 million in credit").

4. Your educational background: name of college (and prep school, if well known), date of graduation and degree, major subjects, advanced degrees, honors and so on.

5. Your professional and community associations and volunteer work, speeches, honors and other items revealing your interests and standing in the world.

6. Your family and personal background: number of children, your age, health (if good) and other kinds of interests: hobbies, jogging, photography, et cetera.

7. Several executive recruiters mentioned that they looked for "knowledgeability"—use of proper buzz words and professional language in the way you express yourself and a warm, human quality.

Characteristics and items that usually raise questions in a résumé

1. Sloppy or overly ornate appearance that suggests a lack of professionalism.

2. Job record with unexplained gaps in the dates. The term *consultant,* often used for periods when the jobholder is out of work or between jobs, may be quite legitimate but must be explained by examples of consulting assignments.

3. Obviously inflated references to your value to the organization or references that may be true in one sense but claim too much (example: "Aided company in setting rec-

189

ord profits during the years of employment'' when your job happened to be assistant to the warehouse manager).

4. Self-praise and vague generalities as to your performance, competence and kind of work. Employers like a résumé that shows a person is self-confident but they are put off by one which suggests vanity or unrealistic ascription of virtues to his person or performance.

5. A "canned" look to the résumé, which suggests it might have been put together by a professional résumé specialist. Employers see thousands of these. Such résumés do not give the reader any sense of the person. Your résumé should in some way reflect your personality.

There is no perfect résumé just as there is no perfect work life, but a carefully tailored résumé, if it is for a job, or one carefully prepared as a general background for yourself, if it is to be a progress report to yourself on your career, is the kind of instrument every jobholder should prepare, whether he or she will use it outside or not. We give below examples of résumés that were successfully used for jobs. They gave their preparers interviews for the kind of jobs they desired.

Strategies for keeping your background current and useful for your own purposes

1. From time to time, every year or so at least, whether you will use it or not outside, prepare a résumé.

2. Whether you use the résumé or not outside, make it as comprehensive as possible. Put in everything about yourself, your jobs, your performances and accomplishments, your outside interests, et cetera.

3. Study this background sheet and see whether it reflects progress in your career and consider how it should look to fully reflect the kind of career you have planned for yourself.

EXAMPLE OF ENTRY-LEVEL RÉSUMÉ

DIANE S. MARTIN

20 Bay Place
Darien, CT 06000   Tel: ____

EDUCATION

Georgetown University School of Foreign Service

Bachelor of Science, 1982, concentration in International Communications, courses included: The Press and Foreign Policy, The Media in American Politics, The Information Revolution and Diplomacy, Dean's List, 1980 and 1982.

University of Dijon France, studies in French language and culture, (May–August, 1980). proficiency in French.

Smith College English major, 1978–1979.

EXPERIENCE IN JOURNALISM AND POLITICS

Assistant to White House Correspondent

Covered White House press briefings and Presidential press conferences (received Secret Service clearance; listed on White House Index). Capitol Hill news reporting. Attended numerous seminars and hearings and provided detailed synopses. Trained in the use of radio broadcast equipment. Organized extensive reference and clipping system. (September, 1981–May, 1982, two days per week.)

Research Intern, The Video Report (WETA)

Developed research briefs on current issues. Monitored Associated Press and Reuters wires. Compiled comprehensive file for interview with Margaret Thatcher at Blair House and composed summary memorandum for Jim Lehrer. (January, 1981–May, 1981, two days per week.)

Legislative Intern to Senator

Evaluated bills and amendments dealing with banking, senior citizens and handicapped issues. Wrote "Dear Colleague" letter

191

and floor speech for banking bill introduced by Senator Weicker. Responded to constituent inquiries. (Summer internships, 1978, 1979. Appointed part-time staff, June, 1979–May, 1980.)

Representative, *Today's World Publishing Company*

Research and development conducted for book on political lifestyles. Arranged and participated in interviews with public personalities. Currently editing and coordinating all publicity for book to be published in 1983. (January, 1979–present.)

PUBLICATIONS

The Hoya, Georgetown University student newspaper, Assistant Features Editor, Contributing Editor and Columnist (1979–1982.)

The Sophian, Smith College student newspaper, Assistant News Editor (1978–1979).

References Available Upon Request

EXAMPLE OF A RÉSUMÉ

VENTURE CAPITAL, INC.

VICE PRESIDENT AND TREASURER—
Chief financial officer of this large company

Background

ROBERT CALLAHAN

12 Bender Lane
Brook Wells, CT

BUSINESS

Venture Capital, Inc.
Venture Capital Plaza
Tel: 000-000-0000

BUSINESS EXPERIENCE

VENTURE CAPITAL, INC.—1972 to present

Vice President, Finance—Chief financial officer of this large venture capital firm, reporting directly to the President

Responsible for all financial functions of the company and certain subsidiaries including the acquisition and divestiture of investments, profit planning, banking relations, cash management, consolidated income tax returns, preparation of stockholder, SEC and SBA reports, insurance and fringe benefits.

BUSINESS ACCOMPLISHMENTS

VENTURE CAPITAL, INC., representative on several boards of directors for both private and public portfolio companies. Acted as chairman and chief executive officer for three of these companies.

- Acquisitions, including a $2,700,000 investment. Responsible for initial review, on-site visitation, negotiation, instructions to attorneys, review of agreements, and closing the investment.
- Negotiated the sale of privately held companies including preparation of offering memoranda, contacting prospective buyers, negotiating terms, instructions to attorneys, reviewing agreements and closing the sale.
- Liaison between Venture Capital, Inc., and portfolio company presidents. Periodic on-site visitations including review of operations and discussions of present and future profitability. Industries involved include aircraft, communications, computer services, cosmetics, electronics, health care, office stationery and supplies, real estate, restaurants and truck service stations.
- Presentation of reports to the VCI Board of Directors, including status of investments, valuation of privately held portfolio companies, proposals for acquisition and divestiture of investments, current financial statements as well as profit and tax forecasts.
- Tax analysis and projections enabling VCI and its 80%-owned companies to generate the maximum advantage out of their complex consolidated tax structure.
- Negotiated a reduction of banks' compensating balance requirement to 5% with funds made available at prime.
- Consultations with outside attorneys, the SEC and the SBA pertaining to accounting aspects of various agreements.

MARBURG MANUFACTURING COMPANY—1968–1972

Treasurer and chief financial officer reporting directly to the Chairman of the Board. Was one of a team of four responsible for running the company, which was sold in 1972. Company manufactured air-conditioner hoses for the automotive industry.

Responsible for all financial functions, including financial statement preparation, profitability and break-even analysis, budgeting, cost accounting, taxes, insurance and cash management.

BUSINESS ACCOMPLISHMENTS:

- Performed systems analysis and restructuring of various departments of the company including production, sales, cost, receiving, shipping and accounting. Made recommendations leading to cost reductions.
- Refined and initiated many computer reports. Coordinated a feasibility study with IBM.
- Negotiated a long-term bank loan and new mortgage.

SMITH & SMITH PUBLIC ACCOUNTANTS—1960–1968

Supervised the audits of listed companies in many industries, including advertising, apparel manufacturing, entertainment, not for profit, paper products, real estate, rubber products, retail and service. Supervised special audits for acquisitions and fraud. Taught internal control seminars.

PROFESSIONAL CERTIFICATION AND MEMBERSHIP:

Certified Public Accountant—New York
American Institute of Certified Public Accountants
New York State Society of Certified Public Accountants
Listed in Who's Who in Finance and Industry and Who's Who in the East

COMMUNITY ACTIVITIES:

Chancellor Commander—Knights of Pythias
Member of the Board of Trustees of Temple
Treasurer local chapter of B'nai B'rith
Coordinator of Eagle Scout Ceremony for Boy Scouts, Member troop
   advisory council

EDUCATION:

Columbia University and City University of New York—MBA Accounting
New York University—B.S. in Business Administration
Elected to Beta Gamma Sigma

PERSONAL DATA:

Married—three children—excellent health.

Executive Recruiters

As you go up in your career, you may receive a call from an executive recruiter. Such a call is a sign of your value and importance in the field in which you work. Executive recruiters are the top search firms, hired by organizations to find executives, professionals or persons with unusual skills for these organizations, and even though you may not be interested in leaving your own organization, it is sometimes worth your while listening to these siren songs. The position may be one you have coveted all your life.

What should you do when the executive recruiter calls?

Here is advice on how to respond from one of the major international executive recruiters, John Wareham, taken from his witty and revealing book *Secrets of a Corporate Headhunter:*

Here's what to do when the headhunter calls:

1. Close your door and listen. Unless you're very comfortable in your present job, this could be a once-in-a-lifetime opportunity.

2. Know who you're talking to before you say anything. A reputable search firm will give its name, and, if need be, you can call them back. You need to be sure that it's a *bona fide* call before you begin to play your hand at all.

3. Once you've established that you are talking to a *bona fide* search consultant (and not your boss), help him. Why shouldn't you? Even if you don't want to explore the opportunity yourself, you may well have an outstanding industry colleague who would like to know about a top opportunity—and he may be in a position to do you a favor himself one day.

4. Handle the call professionally. Even if you're not interested in the opportunity discussed, it could be to your future advantage to impress the caller. Be crisp, efficient, and unfazed by the call. Your phone manner can tell an experienced search consultant more about you than you would believe possible. A good impression could bring him back later with an even more attractive opportunity.

5. Don't ask him how he got your name. Let him assume that you are frequently approached and that you are quite accustomed to such calls. It is testimony to your own high standing in your industry that a headhunter is calling you at all. If you query how or why you are being called, you are querying your own worth.

6. Don't give away confidential information. A good executive is prized for his fine judgment and his ability to handle confidences. If you so much as whisper a word about your present employer's plans, or make any criticism at all, then the consultant will have doubts about you—and rightly so.

7. If you want to explore the opportunity further, then do so in a face-to-face interview. A reputable firm will take even more care of your need for absolute confidentiality than you would yourself. Their reputation is on the line too.

You may well wonder, however, how a headhunter got your name and perhaps how you can get on a top search firm's lists:

—First, of course, you need to have established credentials. You need some degrees, honors, the same kind of credentials that put you on most of the mailing lists for credit cards, investment letters, books, elite stores and the like. You need to get your name into the computers of trade publications, programs, executive lists.

—Next, you should write articles and give speeches. You will then be perceived by competitors in your field as someone to watch.

—Third, get your photograph in the papers for promotions, honors, et cetera. Executive recruiters clip out such items.

—Finally, you may, if you wish, send an original résumé to an executive-recruiting firm in the hopes of an interview, but this is a long shot. It is best that the firm call you. Search firms are working for organizations, not executives who want higher employment. There should be something special about you to receive such a call. One executive-search expert suggests you become a minority candidate, if you can, and if you are a woman, exploit that fact and get yourself interviewed as an example of an executive woman.

Tactics and strategy for when the executive recruiter calls

Again, you may not wish to leave your present organization, but it cannot hurt you to get into the files of a reputable executive search firm. If you accept an interview, here are qualities the executive recruiter will look for to fill important posts:

1. Wear conservative clothes. The recruiter will look for evidence of role awareness—the right clothes, the right manners, the right accent and tone of voice, the right personality for the position and the firm he is recruiting for. The higher the position, the greater the power, the more important will be this aspect of your total package of abilities and qualities.

197

2. Indicate ambition and energy. To succeed in the kind of key position for which such searches are made you need to have a high energy level and be willing to channel it into your job.

3. Make the most of your background—your family background, your parents, your mentors, your ways of looking at the world. Recruiters have to see whether you would fit into the work world of the organization, the kind of people they are, their basic values and orientation.

4. Make the most of your job record in terms of accomplishments. While executive recruiters probably would not have called you unless you had made something of a name for yourself in that field or been recommended by someone of consequence in that field, they nevertheless want to be able to assess your real accomplishments underneath your title and reputation.

5. Indicate your character and loyalty. Have you shown the ability to attract the friendship and respect of your associates and others? Have you shown the ability to be loyal to your job and your organization and to gain the loyalty of those who report to you?

6. Look and act like an executive. Don't try to offer yourself. Take the interview seriously and give information, but you are not there to sell yourself. Recruiters are there to interest you in the beauties of the position being offered. Come across as you are with all your achievements and interests. Ask questions, and as one search executive suggested, you be the one to bring the interview to a close, saying it was a pleasure talking to him or her but you have to get back to work.

Age

There are three periods in your career when age may become a factor in your work life.

The first is the mid-life reassessment, the second, the period when you feel you have gone as far as you can go in your career and third, around age sixty, as you prepare to "retire" from the organization.

That is not to say that age may not at other times be a factor in your work life. As one middle manager commented, "You are always too young or too old—too young for the experience you need to get to the position you want or too old later to move into another career that you might have dreamed of."

As our population has become older and our life-span longer, discrimination because of age has been given almost the same remedies as discrimination because of sex, creed or color. Nevertheless, the problems of age are not normally those caused by the organization but are more likely to be psychological and personal.

The mid-life reassessment

At around age forty most of us are touched by feelings of mortality, by the sudden realization that half our life is over, and a sense that we had better do something about the second half before it is too late. At this period most of us try to reassess our work life, our careers, to see where we have been and where we should be going. It is often at this period that we make changes in our career. We realize that from the work world's perspective, we are at the height of our powers, we are part of the Command Generation, we are mature and experienced enough and vigorous enough to be an asset to any organization in our field. If we feel we have not been sufficiently appreciated or rewarded or that we made a wrong choice, this is the time when we usually consider a major move. Our age is important to us now. We feel this may be our last chance to make the big pitch. We are aware of Time's winged chariot.

Reaching our limit or plateauing out

In our fifties we may come to another milepost where our age is a factor. This is a period most people find difficult to weather—the sense that you have reached your capacities and may not be able to get to the heights you contemplated. Sometimes this arises from your sense that the organization has made this judgment about you, sometimes that you yourself are wanting in certain areas and cannot achieve your ambition.

Preparing to "retire"

The third and most important impact of age on your work usually comes around sixty, when you can see the handwriting on the wall as the normal age of retirement (in most organizations around sixty-five) approaches. Some organizations will then tend to cut down on your assignments or to pass over you for assignments that require longer spans than four or five years. Your successor or successors will become apparent, and you may be asked to train them to take your place. You will usually be given special privileges and regarded much to your chagrin as a grand old man or, more traumatically, as an old man. This is a particularly difficult period, since most of us now remain fully competent and vigorous and our life-spans have so lengthened that the sixties must no longer be considered old but simply late middle-age. We may talk about ourselves as aging but we do not really feel it and we look upon that age landmark with surprise and incredulity. We seem to have come upon it unawares.

Some strategies for surviving those age-related turning points

What can be done about these three age-related periods of our work lives? There are perhaps no hard-and-fast solutions to the psychological impact of such periods, but here are some suggestions, thoughts, and insights gathered from works of psychologists and others who have studied our lives:

1. At the mid-life reassessment it is important not to make purely impulsive and irrational moves. A move may be called for but it should arise from careful and calculated planning. Taking two years off, leaving your organization, adopting a completely different life-style may be what your life needs—or such desires and impulses may be only passing fancies. Patience and planning are the watchwords. One suggestion is to write out the changes you are contemplating and where you hope these changes will take you two to ten years from now. The mid-life reassessment is too important to treat cavalierly or without considerable soul-searching.

2. The "end of the line" syndrome in the fifties is another milestone that must not be treated cavalierly or emotionally. It may well be that you are at a stage where you can enjoy a fulfilling career to retirement despite the prodding of your more youthful ambitions. It may be that you have a way to go to fulfillment and this period is simply a period of discouragement. You must once more look at your career more carefully. Your capacities should not be unfulfilled, but their fulfillment may not necessarily all be within the organization. For most of us, one organization cannot fulfill all of our capabilities or dreams, and despite management's talk of quality of life and job enrichment, fulfilling our dreams is not the organization's responsibility. It is our own. There are outside interests and outside activities that can command all your abilities and powers, many of them volunteer activities that can lead to a later career. You must view your work life as a whole, including interests and activities not connected with one organization, to judge whether you have come to the fullness of the career you have sought.

201

3. Your most important age-related period is in your sixties as you approach retirement. The consensus of those who have studied aging and human life is that no career should be ended at sixty-five, that you should never "retire" in the old sense that you give up meaningful work. Work is a lifelong necessity, like love, and whether the work is for pay or outside the marketplace, it should be important and meaningful to you and call forth your best powers. Those who live long, full lives, according to these professionals, are those who provide themselves with meaningful work to the very end. The surest way to atrophy and grow old before your time is to retire to an extended vacation or a series of meaningless hobbies and waste all the experience and knowledge that your work has given you. In your sixties, say these experts, you must plan for what you will do when you leave the organization where you may have spent most of your work life. You must plan for the rest of what must be a lifetime career.

Each age in the work world has its advantages and its difficulties. Make the most of the advantages.

Benefits

Benefits usually compose as much as 40 percent of your total compensation package in many organizations and they can play a significant role in your life. It is estimated that half the people in private-sector organizations—some 30 million—are covered under benefit plans, and you should be also.

Therefore, as a jobholder, you should know what benefits you have now and what they mean to you. Most benefit packages contain the following items:

—*Contributions to Social Security* (*FICA payroll taxes*). Your employer pays one-half of your Social Security benefit. It is sometimes your most valuable benefit. It is mandated by law.

—*Company pension plans*. These are the most desirable items for most of us in our benefit package. Most companies pay the whole cost of this benefit. It is usually based on length of service and age requirements. After ten years (and sometimes earlier) this pension usually becomes vested and you have a legal right to some pension benefit regardless of any further service under the plan. It is important that you find out exactly what the requirements are in your organization's pension plan.

—*Health insurance plans*. These are often fully paid by your organization. They usually include accident and sickness insurance, long-term disability insurance, and often health insurance for your dependents.

—*Other benefits*. Paid time for holidays (usually ten holidays a year), vacations, personal leave or sick leave.

These are the most common benefits offered. There are other compensation items, such as bonuses and incentive payments, that can be extremely important to you as you go up in the organization. As you approach the top of the organizational ladder, you may be able to work out a favorable contract that gives you stock options and, if your value and position are of great import to the organization, you may be able to work out one of the much criticized "parachute clauses" in your agreement, where, if for any reason you are fired or your services terminated, you will receive a major settlement. These parachute paragraphs are usually only voted to someone whose position is at great risk because of the nature of his commitment (he is brought in to turn around a company in great trouble) or because of a possible loss of the position through merger or acquisition.

Things to consider in your benefit package

Most organizations have booklets describing their benefits to employees, and you should study such a booklet carefully.

If you do not understand any part of the booklet, consult the personnel people.

1. Compare the benefits in your organization with those in the majority of organizations with pension plans. They should include, besides the mandated Social Security, pensions on retirement at age sixty-five or perhaps earlier, health insurance, which includes accident and sickness insurance, long-term disability insurance and often insurance that includes your dependents.

2. Check to see whether some arrangement may be made to include your dependents in your pension plan so that your wife or husband receives the pension for life if something happens to you.

3. Check for any special or unusual benefits such as dental insurance. Check to see what provisions are included in the case of pregnancy and maternity leave.

Surprisingly enough, many jobholders are extremely casual about learning what benefits they are entitled to. Benefits are a very substantial part of total compensation. Learn what they are.

Being Romanced

At the height of your career and from time to time along the way, you may be approached to make a change.

"Harry, if you ever decide to make a move," Otto said, as they sat at lunch, "I hope you'll come and talk to me. You could have a grand future with us."

Harry leaves the lunch greatly exhilarated. Otto is an executive at a rival company. Harry now feels his reputation has gone before him. He is a premium product. If anything happens, he knows he has somewhere to turn.

A year later Harry's organization is taken over by a conglomerate and Harry finds himself out of a job. This time he invites Otto to lunch.

"I'm sorry, Harry," Otto says as they finish dessert. "There doesn't seem to be anything open right now but I'll see what I can do."

Harry is disillusioned. When you don't need them, you're golden, he thinks. When you need them, they don't want you.

This is too often true, and when you are being romanced, you must keep this in mind. You are likely to be romanced when you have a job and at the height of your career, not when you need a job. Furthermore, casual remarks like "Perhaps we can talk about it" or "Stop up and see me if you're contemplating a move" should not be taken too seriously.

That is not to say you should ever completely ignore such invitations. You owe it to yourself and to your career to see what they mean. But as time passes, needs change, and they may want you today but not necessarily next month or next year.

When the executive recruiter calls or when your friend says, "We have something open now. Would you be interested?" then is the time to take matters seriously, to check them out even if you do not intend to move (see "Executive Recruiters" and "The Counteroffer"). Your response, however, should almost always be, "Thanks, I'm not really looking for a change. I'm happy here, but I'll be glad to talk to you."

Being romanced is always pleasant and is to be cherished. But you must not lose your perspective. It is like fame; it can turn a person's head, and then it can leave you high and dry. Take it all with a grain of salt. Be relaxed. The smile of the world, as Chesterton called it, may be on you today and gone tomorrow. Be hardheaded about these offers and keep in mind the virtues of your own organization and your place in it.

Such offers, however, if judiciously revealed, can be used to increase your value in the eyes of your own organization. Unless you are actually contemplating a change, however, you must be careful about using them to increase your salary or push for a promotion. The approach should be, "Can you give me some clue as to my future here and whether there is a possibility of improving my position and salary at this time?"

Strategies to use in dealing with casual offers

1. Being romanced is an opportunity that may come to you at the height of your career. Do not waste it but do not let it lead you to unrealistic hopes or impetuous moves.

2. Check out all offers or suggestions to see how genuine they are and what they really mean.

3. Use such offers judiciously either to better yourself and your career by making the move—always a risk—or by bettering your position in your own organization, if possible.

When to Go

Although this is a guide to keeping a good job, there are situations where you can stay too long, times when you need to consider carefully whether to leave. It is estimated that some eight hundred thousand people change jobs each month—how many voluntarily we do not know, but in many cases a move can be an upward or a life-enhancing requirement.

Here are some common reasons to consider going:

- When your career demands a path that the organization can no longer provide.
- When your usefulness to the organization is at an end.

- When you have an opportunity that your organization cannot match.
- When the culture or style of the organization has changed so drastically that you can no longer fit into it.
- When you are treated unfairly.

When your career path demands it

If your job has become a career, you may reach an impasse in your organization where the kind of skills and experience you need for your career path are not available. You may not even be able to acquire them through outside courses. If the times and the economy make it possible, you should then consider going where opportunity for fulfillment of this career is offered. Be patient, however, and explore with your boss and others in your organization all possibilities before you decide to go.

When your usefulness to the organization is at an end

This is a particularly hard row to hoe, but if you stay too long as a drone, as someone who because of years of service will be kept on in trivial or useless make-work jobs, you will be wasting your most precious asset—your life. Security and making a living are important and essential, but the time may come when you must take a risk to preserve your integrity and your love of life.

When you have an opportunity your organization cannot match

There is always a risk in any change or move, and often what looked like a golden opportunity collapses. Nevertheless, here again you must consider taking the risk. You owe it to yourself, if you wish to fulfill your career and therefore your life, to take the plunge when opportunity opens for you. Try to leave in such a way, however, and with ties of such respect and friendship that, if things do not work out, your organization would be glad to take you back. But whether this is a possibility or not, take the plunge.

When the culture or the style of the organization has changed so drastically you can no longer fit into it

This sometimes occurs when an organization is acquired in a merger or by a conglomerate or when there is a drastic change of management. The organization then brings in people with entirely different goals and skills, and you may find yourself at a long-term disadvantage in this new culture. You are then swimming against the tide, and your chances of succeeding or moving up are slim. You would do well then to consider going.

When you are treated unfairly

From time to time an organization may harbor people with prejudices that militate against you, prejudices that can seriously harm your career. If you are a woman, you may find yourself in an organization that pays lip service to treating all employees fairly but quietly discriminates against women. You may be in an organization where only persons of certain ethnic strains or backgrounds can get ahead or you may finally find yourself in a situation where you have incurred the enmity of someone or some group so powerful that you cannot hope for a fair shake.

If the prejudices result in discrimination so obvious that they can be documented, there are legal remedies (see Part V), but the determining factor, in our opinion, unless you wish to pursue the matter for idealistic purposes or on principle, should be your own self-interest. You are there to make a living and fulfill a career and a life, not to try to change the prejudices of stupid and malevolent people. The better part of valor is usually to go. Litigation is expensive and time-consuming, and unless the rewards are sufficiently large, your best interests will be to opt for the decision to go as soon as possible.

The above are five situations when, despite the advantages of staying with an organization, it is time to go. Difficult as it is to change jobs or to find another job, begin the search when you find yourself in any of these no-win circumstances.

Do not stay too long.

When to Stay

All things being equal, try to stay the course.

There are great advantages in making a career in one organization. You develop friends and reputation. You develop influence and power in proportion to your abilities and personality. Your benefits increase, and you have all the tangible and intangible claims of seniority in the organization.

Nevertheless, when trouble strikes, especially in the early stages of a career, many decide to leave immediately, when, if they were patient, they would find the difficulty to be temporary and they would be on their way again. In our mobile, impatient society, there is often a tendency, particularly among the more gifted jobholders, to jump ship at the slightest setback or to listen to the most specious siren songs and leave.

Here are situations where it may be best to stay, at least to be sure the situation is not just temporary. If you have a good job and you have built a good career for yourself in that organization, why jeopardize it because of a temporary setback? The principle always is: Study the situation carefully, not emotionally, find out the reasons for the setback, and if the situation can be remedied in the long run, be patient. Four common situations to study and, if they are only temporary, to be patient and outwait are:

209

- When a new person whom you dislike has been put in over you.

- When you have been passed over for a raise or promotion.

- When you have asked for a transfer or a different job and been turned down.

- When you feel bored and stymied in your career but do not really know where you want to go.

Strategies and tactics in preserving a job in difficult situations:

When a new person whom you dislike has been put in over you

In almost every career there are times when you may find yourself in a position where a hostile or malevolent boss has been put over you. This is a time to study the situation carefully and to ask yourself some pointed questions: Is it possible you are partly at fault? Can the relationship be put on a stable basis? Is he or she making everybody else miserable also? What chances are there of getting out from under? Will this really affect my whole career here? The last question is the key to your decision. If in the long run this does not seem to affect your goals and career, stay. If the new person is making everyone else miserable also, wait. Such a supervisor is not likely to last long. Meanwhile, see what you can do about a transfer. Personality conflicts are traumatic, but your career is more important.

When you have been passed over for a raise or promotion

Being passed over for one reason or another also seems to occur at least once in most careers, and it is a traumatic, sometimes devastating, experience. But here again it is important to study the situation, not to leave precipitately. One of

210

our advisers told us of the situation in a large professional firm where, at a certain age and with a certain status and experience, an associate could be promoted to partner. One of his better associates was passed over at the June partnership period when he felt he should have received the coveted partnership. He walked into our adviser's office and said, "Well, that's it, Walt. Good-bye."

"Give it some time, Perry," our adviser said, "and let me see what happened or what your prospects are." Within two weeks, however, Perry was gone. Our adviser mentioned the problem to a nominations committee member, who commented, "It's a shame. He would have gotten it next year."

Be patient. Find out what happened, if possible, and if the prospects remain favorable, stay.

When you have asked for a transfer or a different job and been turned down

Unfortunately the organization is not responsible for your career. You are. Sometimes it is not to the organization's interests to transfer you or give you the job you may want at the time you want it. Here again, be patient. You know what you need, and a study of the organization may suggest a way of reaching the position your career demands, if you give the matter enough time and thought. Keep in mind the organization's interests as well as your own and give yourself enough time to see whether these disappointments may not be temporary.

When you feel bored and stymied in your career but you do not really know where you want to go

This is a somewhat common problem in the earlier stages of a job. Most early jobs do not use the full capacities of the jobholder and many of them are boring. The problem, however, cannot be solved unless the jobholder knows what he really wants to do, where he wants to go. Many a lively young person decides to leave the minute the job gets boring or when he or she fails to feel challenged. Going to another job, however, unfortunately will not solve the problem unless you have worked out where you want to go and what you really want to do. This is the major challenge every jobholder faces, and if it is not solved, leaving will not solve it. The problem will be the same in the next job. If you do not know where you are going, until you do, you might as well stay.

Once again, there are situations where you should leave, but, all things being equal, stay. There are many benefits in longevity.

Whom to See

You have decided to make a change. You have another job offer. You are considering leaving a longtime employer. You feel your career demands a change, or, worst of all, you are out of a job, whom do you see?

You need advice and counsel from at least six sources:

- Your family (see "Talking It over with the Family")
- Your mentor (see "Mentor")
- Your friends (see "Lunch with Joe")
- Associations and societies
- Agencies
- People in companies you wish to work for

Your first move is to get the advice and counsel, not to go job hunting or make commitments. Your second and equally important move is to take another fresh look at your career and where you want to go. This is the time to turn change or disaster into opportunity, to reassess your possibilities and make any adjustments to your career path. The adjustments,

212

if any, should probably be up, since most of us are unrealistic in not setting our goals high enough rather than in setting them too high for our capabilities. Your knowledge and experience by this time should give you a realistic picture of where you want to go and how you can get there.

If the change in job puts you into another organization, you will need to seek out those acquainted with this organization's culture as part of your information-gathering process. If you are out of a job, you must work out a plan to see persons in as high a position as you can in organizations you would like to work for. Your network of friends may help you here. You want only to talk to them about that company's business or that field—you are not ready to look for a job yet. If you stress that you are not looking for a job, only for information and give a reasonable purpose, other than job hunting, you may obtain some valuable interviews. Perhaps you are preparing an article on that field or interviewing authorities in companies of this sort for some other legitimate purpose. Information gathering is the key at this stage, and you need to talk to the highest executives possible.

Finally, when you have gathered the kind of information you need to tell you what values your skills and experience might have to those organizations, then you should see the friends, associations and societies and agencies that might advise you in either preparing for the new position or finding the new job. Your chances then are very good either for success in the new position or for finding the new job that you are best qualified for and that you will most enjoy.

Procedures before you make a major change

• You talk to your family first. You outline your plans. You ask them for advice or input. You ask about their goals and interests. You get them behind your plans or modify your plans to take into account their interests.

• You talk to your mentor. If you do not have a mentor,

213

there is usually someone in your old organization whom you admire and who feels friendly toward you and would be willing to advise you or give you information.

• You talk to your friends. You should have by this time built up a network of business friends and acquaintances whom you can contact for advice and information.

• You talk to members of an association or society in your field. You should perhaps be a member yourself. Such an association has a great deal of information on organizations in your field. If you are looking for a job, such associations often have placement committees where you can get leads.

• You talk to employment agencies or executive recruiters, if you can get appointments. It is probably not very effective to send out résumés or background sheets blindly.

• Most important, you attempt to get contacts and appointments with a high executive in the organizations that you want to work for—and to do so first only for information-gathering purposes. You can usually see someone in these organizations if you have a legitimate information-gathering purpose.

Keeping It Quiet

Once it gets around that you no longer want to stay with the organization, your options become limited. No matter how valuable you are, no matter how much the organization wants to keep you, the silver cord is broken by the rumor that you wish to leave. The organization begins to think of surviving without you.

Every organization wants to keep its best people, but the sad truth, which comes home to us all at some time, is that no one is indispensable, that somehow the organization will learn to stagger along without us, and that after we are gone, the waters will close over us, and once our presence is removed, the pool will look much the same.

One would like to believe that the organization will take

extraordinary efforts to keep us if we threaten to leave, and perhaps in some instances this may be the case (see "The Counteroffer"). In many cases also, the organization will make changes, offer a raise or a promotion to induce us to stay, but usually other moves also go into effect. It has been brought to management's attention that the organization may have to get along without us, and since that is part of their job, management must work out how best to replace us, should worst come to worst. So if you use the threat of leaving unwisely or too often, you may find that regretfully, your hand is called and you may not have the winning cards.

This is not to say that organizations do not care whether they keep good people. They must or they will soon go out of business. Certainly their prosperity, if not their survival, depends on it. But that very realization makes them attempt to work out a replacement, where rumor has it or a challenge is made, that you are thinking of quitting. On the other hand, if you are determined to leave, if you have been offered something better and the die is cast, fairness demands that you assist the old organization in replacing you.

Until that time, however, until the die has been cast, for your own sake, keep it quiet. If you confide in anyone, it will be all over the organization or your group before the day is out. Someone may call you in to talk it over, to ask you why you are unhappy or why you are thinking of leaving. You may hear the magic words, "What will it take to keep you?" or you may not. You may hear, "We would hate to have you leave," or you may not. But in any case, steps will probably be taken to fill your place in contemplation of this great loss. And unfortunately tears are quickly dried, and life in the organization will go on.

Tactics and strategies in getting ready to leave

1. Do not paint yourself into a corner by threats to leave.

2. If you contemplate leaving, keep it quiet.

3. If finally you feel you must leave for your own interests, help the organization, insofar as you can, to replace you.

4. Leave the organization on the best possible terms you can. Make them remember you fondly.

Lunch with Joe

"Whatever happened to Cliff Petersen?" Mel asked. "I saw his name in the papers the other day."

"I don't know how he got there, Mel," Joe answered, "but he's beat us all. They made him executive vice-president at Attilla."

"He used to be the guy who'd never go with one of these behemoths. Remember how he hated the Establishment and all those bloated, bloodsucking corporations—especially the oil companies? He was our resident revolutionary."

"I guess it comes to us all, Mel."

"What comes, Joe?"

"Age, Mel. Look at what happened to most of us in the sixties. Hell, I'll bet I'm more radical than Petersen is right now."

"That was some class we had, Joe—noisy, disordered—we messed up the campus good a couple of times."

"They survived, Mel."

"It's a different ball game now, Joe, and I guess we're all out there with the rest, scrabbling for the Establishment. Revolutionaries die young."

"Most of us have families, Mel. Kids and dirty dishes, trying to make a living, does wonders for your perspective, I guess. I wouldn't mind working for Attilla now. They say their salaries and bonuses are terrific. How about your outfit, Mel?"

"Astro is all right. I'm plodding along. No great

216

challenges, but you can count on it and the people are good. It's not like the old class but, as they say, 'It's a living.'"

"I think I'd like to make a change, Mel. There's not much to look forward to at CoCan. You know anybody wants a good, solid engineer, won't start any revolutions?"

"I'll ask around at Astro, Joe. We're doing all right now but, as I say, we're not going to set the world on fire."

"What's happened to Jake Morley?"

"He's with one of the big banks. He's gotten very stuffy."

"He was always kind of serious but he never used to be a phony, Mel."

"I don't know as he's a phony, Joe. It's just that he wants us to think he made it big. Being a vice-president up there, though, isn't in the same ball park as being an executive vice-president at Attilla, you know. Banks have vice-presidents all over the place. Still, he's done pretty well. It's just that he's a pretentious son of a bitch—always was, you remember, always let us know we'd come to no good. He hates Cliff Petersen. Cliff, the old ragamuffin radical, has beaten him at his own game."

"I'll bet Cliff doesn't wear torn pants and a slashed sweatshirt anymore, Mel."

"You'd win, but Cliff is still his own self. He's still a good guy, no side, no bullshit. He's down-home. Why don't you call him, Joe? If there's anything he can do for you, he'll do it. He's helped a lot of us out. Don't let Jake Morley know you're looking, though. It would only give him a chance to crow, but call Cliff—he's got a lot of clout and I'll bet he'll find something for you."

"Thanks, Mel."

Talking It over with the Family

In the old days the man's career came first. No longer. The interests of the family—the wife's job or community interests, the children's schooling, friends, the depth of roots in the community—weigh equally in major job decisions. A job is a job, but a life is a life.

If you decide to take a transfer, if you decide to leave the job or to take another kind of job, talking it over with the family first has become important. A person's job is the family's business as well as its livelihood, and this is just as true in the two-paycheck family, where the wife also has a job and a career.

In good times and bad, changes in a job are traumatic. Hard times can force you out of a job and into the job market. Good times can offer you an opportunity you would not wish to refuse. In either case you must sit down with the family and work out a plan that will, insofar as possible, protect the interests of the others who are dependent on you.

Strategies and tactics to deal with job changes

The plan must, of course, be tailored to the circumstances, but these are the questions that must be addressed:

—What about the spouse's career? What impact will the change have on it, and how can things be so arranged that the change does not damage the spouse's interests and ability to sustain his or her career?

—What impact will the change have on the children's education? If the change is a transfer, are the schools in the new neighborhood adequate? If the change is brought about by hard times and the children must be taken from a private school to go into a public school, what will be the effect and how can they be prepared for it?

—What objections and qualms do members of the family

have, if the change is a transfer or a different job, and how can they be brought out, worked out and put to rest?

—If the change is a loss of a job, how best can the family be prepared for the times ahead and how can you prepare yourself to handle the hard job of finding another job?

—How can communication and sharing of plans and problems be maintained over the period of change?

When a change is to be made in your career, good or bad, it is important for both yourself and the members of your family that you do not try to bear it alone. It is important that you talk it over with the family, that you get their input and that whatever changes must be made are fully understood and agreed upon. Bad times can be weathered with the family, and good times must be shared.

Talk it over.

Letting Them Know

You have decided to take that other job. You have said yes. You have made the commitment.

Now you must play fair with your old company. You must let them know you have decided to leave and why. You must give them time and, if possible, help them to replace you. You cannot leave overnight.

"When can you start?" the other company's executive has asked you. It is August 15.

"Would October 1 be all right?" you answer.

"Can't you make it a little earlier? We need you right now. Tomorrow, in fact."

The correct answer is, "I'm afraid not. I have a number of things I have to finish in this job, and it looks to me as if October 1 is the earliest I can start. Perhaps I can stop over from time to time between

219

now and then and talk to you and others about my duties."

"All right, Jim," the executive of the other company says. "October 1, it is. Meanwhile, I'd like you to talk to Jack Marsh in Personnel and get some of the preliminaries squared away."

Now you are ready to let them know in your old company and you have given them a month and a half if they want it to adjust to your leaving and to find a replacement.

What kind of reception will you get?

This, of course, depends on your relationship with the organization and its people and your contribution and length of service. If you are valuable, the news will be received with genuine regret and good wishes. There may be a counteroffer, and this adds to your problems in leaving (see "The Counteroffer").

In any event, you will ask how soon it would be convenient for you to leave and whether there is anything you can do to help them replace you.

This is one way to leave right (see "Leaving Right").

The Counteroffer

Executive recruiters, who have worked hard to position you in the new job that you agreed to try for, are justifiably fearful of the counteroffer.

One executive recruiter told us this story:

Jim Collier had been somewhat dissatisfied with his job at Conglomerate, Inc., and when we approached him for a high position in one of the Fortune 500 companies, he agreed to present himself for it. After six months of extensive interviews and the consideration of five other candidates, the company finally selected Jim for the position of vice-president of Information Services.

Jim went to his boss, the executive vice-president of Conglomerate, Inc., and informed him that he had decided to take a position in another company because he felt he had more future there and they were offering him an increase in salary and stock options and other inducements.

His boss, Joe Fisher said, "Jim, what will it take to keep you here? We can meet all their offers, and I have great plans for you in the near future."

Jim was flattered. No one had paid much attention to him in higher management until then and there had been no evidence that there were plans for him. "What were the plans?" he remembered to ask. Joe gave him some vague answer, which seemed to indicate that they were just being formulated. Jim said, "Let me think it over." That night he talked it over with his wife. His wife listened. "Maybe I shouldn't leave," he said.

"Finally, he came to us," the executive recruiter explained, "and said he had decided to stay. Six months later, he was on the phone with me again. 'I made a mistake,' he told me. 'If you have anything for me, I'd appreciate it.'"

This happens frequently, one executive recruiter told us. The situation that prompted the executive to search for another job did not really change, even though his employer met the other company's offer financially.

The moral of the story:

Be sure you know what you are seeking in accepting another position.

If it is simply to be used as a way of improving your position in your own firm and it works, fine.

If it is to place yourself higher and to meet the demands of a career path, then do not be swayed by the counteroffer. If your standing in your company does not satisfy you and they seem to have no future plans for you, this is not likely to change, even if they meet an offer financially.

221

Becoming a Consultant

The dream of many of us is someday going into business for ourselves, and this translates itself into two possibilities: becoming an independent consultant or starting a small business of our own (see "Going into Business for Yourself"). For most of us these two possibilities remain dreams, but they are alternatives not to be overlooked, if age or other factors have stalled your career or if your talents and experience are such that they may be packaged for a market.

Let us look first at the challenges of becoming a consultant. We will listen to Richard F. Creedy, who has been a successful consultant for eighteen years. He quit his job as copy chief of a major advertising agency and became an advertising consultant.

"Based on my experience," Dick Creedy told us, "I think the clue to starting out on your own as a consultant is to do some careful planning by asking yourself four key questions.

First, "What is it that I have to offer?"

To answer this, consider your knowledge, your experience or some of the duties in your current job.

One young woman used her knowledge of where to buy things and her keen interest in shopping to open a thriving interior decorating service. A businessman used his traveling experience to start a service of chauffeuring people's cars to their vacation homes. An employee who prepared detailed drawings in an architectural firm turned this skill into a full-time business of providing drawings for a number of different firms.

When examining your personal skills, look for the obvious things you do well. Your objective is to define a service based on your own strengths so you can sell it with confidence.

The market

The second question you need to answer when starting out is, "Who will buy my service?"

222

Here you need a clear definition of your marketplace so you can deal with the real world. For instance, if you are good at doing market research, you will need a specific group of people who will buy that service. Maybe they are all in real estate or in accounting firms.

You will need to know who and where they are and what they want to buy. Profit often hinges on the difference between being specific and vague about your marketplace.

The third question is, "What will my service cost?"

To answer this, you should focus on your continuing overhead costs.

For your new business you will probably require some professional equipment, including perhaps a typewriter, an adding machine, some reference books, a telephone and maybe a phone answering service and some stationery supplies.

You can keep your costs down by working out of your home. Or you might move into a small office with a friend and even exchange your services on an hourly basis for rent.

If you are careful, your total start-up expenses may be only a few hundred dollars.

Earning power

The fourth question is simply, "What can I earn?"

If you work on a time basis, here is how to figure your earning power. After subtracting vacations, weekends, holidays, and nonbillable days (used for selling and administrative work), you wind up with about 200 billable days a year. If you charge—let's say—$50 an hour and successfully sell these 200 billable days, you will earn $70,000. Of course, it will take time to earn this kind of money, but it can be done.

In establishing an hourly rate, you should keep in mind what goes inside this rate: 30 percent for overhead, 25 percent (or more) for taxes, and 45 percent for salary and profit.

Your purpose is to develop a profitable hourly rate and learn to make it work.

In addition to these basic questions, here are a few pitfalls to avoid!

Don't be casual about running your business or you'll never know whether it is profitable, and you'll probably wind up in the red.

Don't try to fake knowledge you don't have. Find it in a book. Or get help from the right person, whether it be an accountant, a banker, or a lawyer. Most important of all, take courses in a continuing education program to prepare yourself and keep yourself up-to-date in your field.

Running your own business of selling your professional skills offers exciting opportunities. I happen to think that anyone can do it successfully if he or she plans carefully, focuses on some basic questions, remembers some "don'ts"—and keeps in mind some words of advice from Ben Franklin.

Back in 1748 Franklin wrote a letter to a tradesman. In it he said, "Remember that time is money. Waste neither time nor money, but make the best use of both."

In eighteen years of running my own business, I have found this to be solid advice.

Strategies and tactics in becoming a consultant

Supplementing Dick Creedy's invaluable advice, keep some of the problems in mind:

1. Building a list of clients takes time. You must give yourself at least half a year to attract a good, solid client to pay your overhead.

2. If you do decide to try going out on your own, try to get your old organization to become your first client. After all, they know you and what you can do for them, and if your relationship has been good, they may be able to

make a consulting arrangement with you. This will get you off to a good start.

3. Relationships become of major import in a client-consulting arrangement. You must learn not just to tolerate but actually to enjoy your clients if you are to be successful as a consultant.

4. You will have to have self-confidence and maturity to weather the lean periods when no one seems to need you.

5. You will have to be continually abreast of what is going on in the market for your services and stay up-to-date in your particular expertise.

Going into Business for Yourself

Every year some five hundred thousand new businesses are started in the United States. Some of these survive, and a few of these make their owners rich. Most of them are experiences of life and devotion that cannot be duplicated in any other way in a lifetime. If you are of an entrepreneurial or adventurous temperament, if you want, as they say, to be your own boss, this may be the answer.

There are, however, some drawbacks you should know about:

• You are taking a major risk. Of the five hundred thousand businesses started each year, some four hundred thousand fail. Nearly half of these ventures fail in the first year, and 80 percent of them do so in the first four years. The chief cause of failure is generally lack of a sound plan and not understanding management techniques.

• The hours are rarely nine to five. They are often ten to twelve hours a day, weekends and a lot of sleepless nights.

• You are going to have to learn everything about a business, not just about the product or service you are marketing. You are going to have to learn accounting and finance, production and distribution, marketing and selling and, if you bring in others, human relations.

• You are going to have to begin by doing almost everything yourself and not depend on others to get anything done. Then, as the business grows, you are going to have to unlearn doing everything yourself and begin to delegate and trust others.

• You are going to have to learn to plan.

But the rewards are fantastic and almost indescribable:

• You are creating something that, though there may be a thousand similar organizations around, is yours alone. This is akin to the artist creating a work of art. It will express everything that is within you.

• You are in a sense your own man. You may sometimes be at the beck and call of customers or clients who can be much more demanding and fickle than any boss, but if you run your business right, no one customer or client can put you out of business, and usually you can choose your customers or clients and those you want to deal with.

• You can get rich. Entrepreneurs make big money more often than do salaried employees.

Some steps to take if you are going into business for yourself

Assuming that this is a viable possibility for you, what steps should you take? Your first and most important step is a business plan.

The business plan will be the instrument by which you raise money for the business, unless all its financing is coming from you and your family, and if that is the case, you owe it to yourself and your family to prepare such a plan. It will be a guide to you in setting up the business, in keeping its objectives in view and even in operating it.

226

Here are the elements you will need in your business plan:

1. A description of the business.
2. The market for the product or services.
3. The competition.
4. The rationale for the location of the business.
5. The management—that is, how you are going to run it.
6. The people involved and their backgrounds.
7. How the money will be spent—how you intend to allocate your resources and what effect each form of allocation is expected to have on the success and profitability of the firm.
8. A balance sheet forecast.
9. An income statement forecast.

The most complete guide to starting a business that we know of is a two-volume series entitled *Money & Your Business—How to Get It, How to Manage It, How to Keep It* by Robert E. Butler and Donald Rappaport, partners of Price Waterhouse, published by the New York Institute of Finance (see "Suggested Reading").

Going into business for yourself is not for everyone. The costs are as high as the possible rewards. One of the costs you must take into account is that your family must pay for your going into business for yourself. Your wife or husband is going to have to support you in any such adventure, because work of this sort requires an extraordinary charge on your time, energy and devotion.

What You Can Take with You and What You Cannot Take with You

You are leaving the organization. It is your last week, and you must pack up and get your things out of the old office.

This is an emotional period. You have been there for a few years, and it is amazing what you have accumulated. A lot of the old material can be dumped. This place had become a home to you, and there is a lot of personal stuff also. It is true there are many things you would like to take with you, that may be useful to you in your new job. Yet even if you feel the old organization has not been fair to you or you are leaving for good reasons, your integrity and honesty are on the line. There are things you can take with you and there are things you cannot take with you. An organization has confided a great amount of confidential and proprietary material to a trusted executive, and whatever your feelings about the organization, you must respect its property and confidence in you.

What you can take

- memories
- knowledge
- experience
- expertise
- personal papers
- evidence of your own work, if not confidential
- honors and accolades bestowed on you
- friendships
- mementos and photographs
- descriptions of operations and campaigns mentioning your name that are not confidential
- information that could be helpful in your next job that is not confidential or proprietary
- publications available to the public
- letters of commendation or appreciation of your work
- company-property items that you have permission to keep

What you cannot take

• confidential or proprietary material, including memoranda, reports, blueprints, schematics, models, plans and other such material that the organization would not wish to have fall in the hands of competitors or the public

• company property, unless with permission

• reports sent to you by other members of the organization that though not confidential might reflect on the organization, unless with permission of the sender

In addition to the things you cannot take, there are things you cannot use in the service of your new employer without possibly making you and your present employer liable—such matters as trade secrets or reproduction of a proprietary product so similar to your former employer's that it could be considered infringement of patent.

In the present complex world economy, industrial espionage has become a problem. In the work world many instances of it have been recorded in court papers of engineers, technical people and others hired solely for their knowledge of proprietary material.

If you leave, remember the things you can take with you and the things you cannot.

Corporate Cultures

There has been a spate of studies of what has been perceived and identified more and more as the "corporate culture." In these studies the shared values, aspirations and customs of the organization are usually described as its culture. In one book, *Corporate Cultures: The Rites and Rituals of Corporate Life*, the authors, Terence E. Deal, Ph.D., and Allan A. Kennedy, contend that corporate culture is generally the result of current management philosophy, and they have grouped management philosophies into four types, which produce four generic cultures.

These cultures are determined primarily by two factors of the marketplace:

- The degree of risk in the enterprise.

- The speed of feedback on success of decisions or strategies.

Based on measuring these two factors, Deal and Kennedy found they could define the four kinds of corporate culture as follows:

CORPORATE CULTURES DEFINED

- The tough-guy, macho culture, characterized by high risks and quick feedback on whether actions were right or wrong. Within this category are construction, cosmetics, management consulting, venture capital and the entertainment industry.

- The work hard/play hard culture, typified by sales organizations, where employees take few risks, with quick feedback.

- The bet-your-company culture, a high-risk, slow-feedback environment. Organizations here are large-systems businesses, oil and mining companies, investment banks, architectural firms and computer-design companies.

- The process culture, where employees find it hard to measure what they do, so they concentrate on *how* it's done. Examples are banks, insurance companies, utilities and government agencies.

In considering whether you are in the right organization for your temperament and success potential, you may want to see which category of corporate culture your company most nearly approximates (see also Part III, "The World According to the Company" and "The World According to the Boss").

Why Some Made It and Why Some Did Not

Luck—being at the right place at the right time—and major abilities are important, but why then, even with these two essential ingredients, do some go to the top, while others do not?

Two behavioral scientists, Morgan W. McCall, Jr., and Michael M. Lombardo of the Center for Creative Leadership in Greensboro, North Carolina, made a study with their associate Ann Morrison of forty-one executives slated for the top—twenty of whom made it, twenty-one who did not.*

The researchers used the judgments of highly placed, influential and experienced insiders in several Fortune 500 companies to make the judgments on men they knew well as to why twenty of these executives succeeded and twenty-one were, as they put it, "derailed." These sources mentioned some sixty-five factors which the researchers boiled down to ten categories of "fatal flaws" that seem to have been involved in the failure to reach the top. What were these fatal flaws?

The one most often mentioned was insensitivity to others. Below is the list of flaws that sealed the fate of those who fell short of ultimate success:

EXECUTIVE FATAL FLAWS IN TWENTY-ONE WHO DID NOT MAKE IT TO THE TOP

1. Insensitive to others: abrasive, intimidating, bullying style.
2. Cold, aloof, arrogant.
3. Betrayal of trust.
4. Overly ambitious: thinking of next job, playing politics.

* *Psychology Today*, February 1983.

5. Specific performance problems with the business.
6. Overmanaging: unable to delegate or build a team.
7. Unable to staff effectively.
8. Unable to think strategically.
9. Unable to adapt to boss with different style.
10. Overdependent on advocate or mentor.

It was not that those who succeeded did not have flaws or conversely had all the virtues of major abilities, it was that they managed to avoid those flaws that stop a person from growing or learning and that turn others against them: insensitivity, arrogance, inability to listen, one-upping, ambition that blinds them to the needs and desires of other people. Without sensitivity to others, it appears, the person stops growing or learning.

In those who failed, this blindness and arrogance generally led to performance flaws from not being able to work with experts or from not being able to motivate those who reported to them. Others in their ruthlessness in the high-pressure, demanding world of upper management, where to be able to trust others is a necessity, committed that one unforgivable sin: they betrayed a trust, they broke a promise.

In other areas, this lack of ability to grow turned early strengths into weaknesses: simple ambition became Machiavellianism, politicking; loyalty turned to cronyism; trying to please superiors turned to ruthlessness toward those below them. Those who succeeded made many mistakes, some of them serious, but they seemed able to learn from them; they were able to grow in the face of adversity.

The authors of the study came to the following conclusions in comparing those who succeeded and those who were derailed:

> Although neither group made many mistakes, all of the arrivers handled theirs with poise and grace. Almost uniformly, they admitted the mistake, forewarned others so

232

they wouldn't be blind-sided by it, then set about analyzing and fixing it. Also telling were two things the arrivers didn't do: They didn't blame others, and once they had handled the situation, they didn't dwell on it . . .

One of the senior executives we interviewed made a simple but not simplistic distinction between the two groups. Only two things, he said, differentiated the successful from the derailed: total integrity and understanding other people.

They concluded, however, in these words:

The reasons that some executives ultimately derailed and others made it all the way up the ladder confirm what we all know but have hesitated to admit: There is no one best way to succeed (or even to fail). The foolproof, step-by-step formula is not just elusive; it is, as Kierkegaard said of truth, like searching a pitch-dark room for a black cat that isn't there.

Adventure

Ron Bevin is a vice-president in a bank in a Midwest city. He is a loan officer and through his good judgment has been responsible over the years for the growth of a number of small businesses in that city and has made many friends in the twenty years he has been a banker to people with small businesses.

He considers himself an old-fashioned banker, the kind who in the consideration of the Three C's in banking—character, competence and collateral—places equal emphasis on character, an emphasis he feels has in late years become unfashionable. But under his businesslike exterior beats the heart of an adventurer, and now that he is approaching retirement, he has decided he will prepare for it by doing at least two of the things he has always wanted to do. He is going to build a house and he is going to have tea at the North Pole.

Ever since he read the brochure of a small airline that takes tourists over the North Pole and, in the words of the brochure, "weather permitting" will go down at the North Pole for tea, this is one of those things he wants to do before he dies.

When we talked to him about the work world and his job, we found he had decided his career was far enough along so that he would have to embark on these two adventures.

"There's an old Chinese saying," he told us, "that goes: 'A man must do three things before he dies: father a child, build a house and write a book.' I may never get the book written, but I have the pleasure of children, and, by God, I'm going to build a house. I've bought three acres in the country, and that's where I'm going to be weekends and when I retire. But right now I'm going to do a fourth thing that old Chinese in his wisdom had not contemplated: I'm going to have tea at the North Pole."

Ron Bevin is sixty years old but he has stayed young. The job was one adventure. And he is never going to let adventure out of his life.

Stay young.

Have tea at the North Pole.

Leaving Right

Bob Simmons walked into Josh Taylor's office. He simply could not stand being with the organization one more day. He felt the strain and anger were beginning to undermine his health, and he was convinced that because of the confining nature and long hours of the job, he would never be able to find another job unless he quit and devoted himself full-time to it.

Josh was a deceptively pleasant-looking middle-aged man, but a bully and a hard taskmaster. He leaned back in his chair and contemplated Bob with hard, glittering eyes:

"I don't remember your having an appointment with me, Simmons," he said. "To what do I owe this intrusion?"

"You don't think I would find any pleasure in coming to see you unless it were something important, Taylor," Bob said. "I've come to tell you I'm quitting. You can take this crummy job and shove it up your ass. I've been here two years and I don't know how I've stood it. I don't know how anybody stands it. This is one of the shabbiest, most depressing organizations I've ever seen. The conniving, the politicking, the knifing of people behind their backs is sickening. My desk is cleared out. I will be out of here before lunch. I just wanted to tell you to your face what I think of you and what everyone else thinks of you. I think you're a shit and I don't want any part of you. Good-bye."

As you may imagine, this is not quite the right way to leave a job.

As indicated, our advisers emphasize that you should think long and hard before leaving the job you have. They recommend also that, unless circumstances force you to, you do not leave the job you have until you have landed another job.

If, as in the case of Bob Simmons, you feel you must leave the job before you find another, you should realize that finding a new job is a major task and may take months. Robert Half of the Half Agency has developed a job-search time guide based on a minimum of one week for every $2,000 of salary and bonus you receive. Thus, if you were making $30,000 a year, salary and bonus, it should take you a minimum of fifteen weeks to find another job of the kind you have. But there are other elements to take into consideration:

Competition. If your skills are rare and in demand, you can deduct 20 percent from the base time; if commonplace and not in great demand, you must add 50 percent to the base time.

Exposure. If you must keep your search a secret for any reason (as when looking while you still have the old job), this doubles the time it will take you.

Needs. If you demand specific location, type of work, size of company, et cetera, you must add 20 percent to the search time.

Salary. If you are asking for more salary than you were or are receiving, you must double your search time.

During recession and hard times, of course, even these estimates may be optimistic.

But assuming you are in a position intolerable to you, as in the case of Bob Simmons, even so, there is a right way to leave a job. In principle you should leave a job on as pleasant and warm a basis as you can, no matter what the feelings and emotions that may have caused you to consider the change.

Some strategies on leaving

1. Avoid criticizing the organization. Even if asked why you are leaving, avoid listing the defects of the present organization or even the real reason if it is owing to serious defects of your present job.

2. Emphasize only the positive advantages the new job offers and indicate a regret that you must leave.

Is It Worth It?

Most of us during our work life ask ourselves a number of times whether all the struggle and maneuvering, all the long days and late hours, the stings and arrows of politicians, the authoritarians, the hostilities, all the competition, the drudgery and the boredom have been worth it.

And most of us in the end have to give the same answer we would give if we were asked, "Is life worth living?" That answer for almost all of us would be yes and often a resounding yes.

Furthermore, in the work world where we have spent most of our lives, things are changing—and for the better. These changes are of three kinds: those affecting the jobs themselves, those affecting us as jobholders and those affecting the work environment.

The jobs

Jobs have become more varied and complex, more interesting and challenging. You have to know more to get them and learn more to keep them. The white-collar, service, professional and managerial jobs are becoming the dominant occupations in our society; unskilled and blue-collar jobs seem to be fading. Census reports show the following occupations to be on the rise:

JOBS ON THE RISE

Occupation	Percent Increase
Computer operators	346.2
Teachers' aides	190.2
Social scientists	155.0
Health administrators	150.0
Roofers	139.7
Sales demonstrators	139.5
Real estate agents	122.1
Bank tellers	113.3
Restaurant and bar managers	108.7
Receptionists	106.9

The following occupations seem to be going out of fashion:

JOBS OUT OF FASHION

Occupation	Percent Decrease
Tailors	61.2
Stenographers	50.0
Newspaper vendors	39.6
Barbers	35.3
Textile operatives	24.9
Garage workers	22.9
Telephone operators	22.5
Tool and die makers	12.9
File clerks	10.0
Sewers and stitchers	9.3

Source: "U/S: A Statistical Portrait of the American People," by Andrew Hacker.

The *U.S. Standard Occupational Manual*, published by the Department of Commerce, identifies some six thousand kinds of jobs in the United States. Most of these are in the white-collar, service and administration areas, reflecting the increasing sophistication and complexity of our economic life and standards of living.

We as jobholders

The U.S. work force has risen dramatically in the last decade. Some 26 million people entered the work world, bringing the total to around 100 million. The most dramatic change was the huge influx of women. By 1982 fully 52 percent of the female population were in the work world outside the home, and the two-paycheck family had become a commonplace. Women were also rising in the professions and more slowly in management. Fully 67 percent of the women between the ages of eighteen and thirty-four were in the labor force by 1982,

238

while the participation of men in the work world had fallen from 87.3 percent in 1951 to 77 percent in 1982. The great influx of those born during the Baby Boom years entering the job market in the 1970s lowered the average age of those working from thirty-nine to thirty-four years and created heavy competition for jobs, intensifying the agonizing problem of unemployment in the early 1980s.

The work environment

The work environment nevertheless has improved in the last two decades. Those of us who hold jobs now live in a far less authoritarian cnvironment than that of even a decade ago. Organizations find themselves requiring more highly educated and sophisticated people, who demand some participation in managing and defining the job, who tend to resent an authoritarian approach and who insist on a voice in any matters in the work world that affect them. There is a far greater tolerance for individualism and personal goals and desires. There is, in fact, a greater respect for the individual in the work world. Even in the legal structure of our society, certain claims of the individual with respect to his or her job are beginning to be recognized. We are still somewhat behind Western European countries in the protection given by custom and law to jobholders' rights as an employee, but the trend, if not allowing the jobholder to "own" his job, is at least toward giving the employee certain rights in it and to some degree giving the person protection from losing a job under certain circumstances. The legal aspects of such kinds of protection will be shown in Part V, "Legal Remedies," through the stories summarized in key court cases.

There is nothing more fun or more deeply fulfilling than a good job, and there is only one thing worse and more destructive than a bad job, and that is no job.

Retiring

Here are two retirement stories:
Fred Langdon was an executive vice-president of a large company. Board members gave a retirement dinner for him.

"What are you going to be doing, Fred?" his friend Art Connolly asked.

"I'm going fishing, Art," Fred said. "I've had all the pressure I need for the rest of my life. Now I'm just going to take it easy."

"Fred," said Sid Brown, a fellow board member, "would you be interested in serving on a committee over at Starborough?"

"Sorry, Sid," Fred said, "no more committees, no more meetings, no more involvements for me. I've sat through all the meetings I'm ever going to sit through. My main occupations from now on are eating and sleeping."

"What are you really going to do, Fred?" Cole Martin asked.

"You guys don't believe me, but I'm telling you. I'm going to get to know my wife and, while my sons are grown and gone, I'll be visiting them and spoiling the grandchildren."

Seven years later Fred Langdon died at the age of seventy-two. He was very fat and had grown querulous and cantankerous. His wife, in his words, had more or less left him. As she had said, she was not used to having him underfoot and she had had her own life, her community and volunteer activities, which were important to her. Also, as she had commented to Fred, "I married you for better or for worse but not for lunch."

As he had become more lethargic, she had become more active. As he seemed to have grown much older, she seemed to have grown much younger. His life seemed to him to have closed in. The world seemed to him to have grown much less interesting and much more dangerous and stupid—everything deteriorating, violence increasing, people more callous, ignorant and self-centered. He had begun to hate to get up in the morning. His weight had become a serious problem, and one afternoon as he was puffing up the beautiful curved stairway of his large house, his heart gave out and the show was over.

The other retirement story concerns Stephen Bremerton, partner in a prestigious law firm in Washington. His retirement was also celebrated by his partners. He had been an extremely active, highly regarded practitioner in corporate law with many international clients.

> "What are you going to do now, Steve?" Jim Manion, one of his partners, asked.
> "You'll laugh if I tell you, Jim," Stephen said.
> "You going into practice again somewhere?" Jim asked.
> "Where Millie and I are going to settle down I doubt they need any international corporation lawyers," Stephen said. "I guess I'll be the only partner of our grand old firm who'll end up pumping gas for a living."
> "You're joking."
> "No, Millie and I took a vacation once in a little village near São Paulo. I bought a gas station there as an investment. We're going back to work on our investment and to live the village life that we enjoyed so much. There may be other things, but that's what we're going to try first."

Here is a letter from Stephen Bremerton's son, who went down to visit him eight years later:

> "My father bought the gas station because when he and my mother stayed in that village one summer it looked like a good investment.

241

"It was. Over the years, by adding more pumps, increasing ramp space, adding a garage with hydraulic lifts for oil changes and working sixteen-hour days, they increased sales by nearly 600 percent to 450,000 gallons per year. Gasoline sells for the equivalent of $2.53 per gallon. Pure alcohol, another widely used motor fuel, sells for $1.49.

"My father says fast, friendly service and the little extras like candy for customers' children have also been big factors in the increased sales.

"My mother 'lends' some of her time from the real estate business to help with the bookkeeping at the station. Her biggest job is handling the rivers of cash that pass through the station. Sometimes she makes five or six deposits a day at the banks.

"She recently invented a coin-counting machine to handle all the coins they receive, mainly from bus drivers who pay with the day's fares. A patent was secured, and plans are being made to market it nation-wide. The machine is inexpensive, accurate and breaks down less often than the big mechanical ones in use in Brazil today. She believes many banks will be interested.

"Running a gas station in a small, rural Brazilian town is not quite like operating one in downtown São Paulo. Townspeople stop to chat and drink the freshly brewed coffee my mother always has sitting on the counter. Free of charge, of course. Vendors often call, selling lemons, fruits and raw honey. My mother has the final say as to whether or not to buy, but not before everybody in sight has gathered around to add their two cents. They maintain accounts at six banks in town, to keep everybody happy. Occasionally their dog follows them to the station and spends the day snooping around town or sleeping contentedly under my mother's desk.

242

"Between running two businesses, employing more than ten people, consulting and inventing, my parents have time for little else. They are not the kind of people to sit at home and reminisce. Not while they still have time to create another lifetime of memories."

The names have been changed, the identities concealed, but both stories are true. The Bremertons knew how to retire.

SELF-ASSESSMENT ON PART IV, "THE OUTSIDE WORK WORLD"

Keeping a perspective, keeping a window open on the world is important to you in your job and in your career. These questions will test you on your handling of situations where this perspective, this knowledge of the outside work world, play an important role in your success in your career and in your life. Relevant discussions are indicated in suggested answers and references to these self-assessment questionnaires on pages 279–284.

1. You have been immersed in a demanding though challenging and interesting job for the last five months. Then one day, after an exhausting week of ten-hour days, you look up and realize that that particular project will be complete in another month and you will be back to the relatively humdrum routine before the project began. You wonder whether you can go back to the old routine. What do you do?

2. You have learned a great deal on that demanding project. You wonder whether the new skills you have gained make you more valuable, put you at a higher level? What should you do to find out?

3. You talk over with your boss whether you might be worth a bit more now that you've finished this major project. He says you're at the top of your salary range and these are hard times. He says to be patient. What should you do?

4. You have been with your present organization six months and you hear of a great opening you are pretty sure you could fill, and besides, this job, like the one before and the one before that, has become boring. The thrill is gone and most of your associates are jerks and you are generally unappreciated. Should you try for this new opening?

5. You have been passed over for a promotion. Up to this time things had gone pretty well, but you are hurt and disappointed. One of your friends at another company indicates that there may be an opening there in a similar job. You investigate and receive an offer. Should you go?

6. You have come to a crossroads in your career. You have been with the same organization for eleven years. You do not see exactly where you are going or what you have accomplished. What is one of the first things you can do that can help you take a look at your career?

7. You hear a voice on the phone saying, "We are searching for someone to fill a high position in your field in a Fortune 500 organization, and your name was given us as someone who might help us. Could you give me a minute of your time?" What do you say?

8. A friend in a small, struggling company offers to hire you as a consultant to help on the weekends and some evenings in working out a manufacturing production schedule. You are an engineer in a big electronics company, not making the same kind of product, and you are not in

the manufacturing area of your company. Can you take
this consulting job on the side?

9.   Another friend calls and says, "We need someone like
you over here. If you ever think of making a change,
how about coming over and talking to me?" You are
satisfied in your present job but intrigued. How should
you respond?

10.   You have been in the same job for eleven years. You like
the job fairly well and are comfortable in it. You like
your associates and the organization, but this is not anywhere near where you thought you might be by this time
and you are asking yourself whether this is the way it is
going to be to the end of the line. You look at the organization and you look at yourself and you see a good
enough fit, but you do not see them needing you or wanting you in any further position or at any higher level.
And frankly you are beginning to be a little bored. What
should you do?

11.   A new manager has been brought in over you. He prom-
ises to clean up what he terms the slackness and sloppi-
ness of the division's operations. He is abrasive, cantankerous and demanding. You go home each evening
fantasizing ways of killing him that include the most agonizing torture and humiliation. You begin to lie awake
nights mulling over the injustice of it. You know you
have done a brilliant job, and until this monster was
placed over you, your prospects seemed exceptionally
bright in the organization. What do you do?

12.   You have decided to make the move. You have all but
made the commitment. You are wondering whether to
let them know about it now. It would be only fair, you
think. After all, they've been good to you, and making
the move is not because of anything wrong with the organization but because you feel your future demands it.
What should you do?

13. You have been offered a tremendous job at the head-
     quarters of the organization in a distant city. Your salary
     and stock options and other benefits will be sufficient to
     assure a very comfortable life even if your wife gives up
     her job in her boutique, an enterprise she has established
     over eight years and which is now becoming successful.
     The children, however, are finally settled in an excellent
     school and with many friends, and your family has de-
     veloped deep roots in the community. What should you
     do?

14. You go to see your boss to tell him you have decided to
     make a move. You have been happy there, you say, but
     an executive recruiter has called, and another position at
     a higher level with more money has been offered. Your
     boss says, "We can meet any offer you've been given,
     and furthermore, though I can't divulge plans now, we
     may have great things in store for you." What should
     you do?

15. You have been working in the financial area of an old-
     line insurance company. You are offered a job in the
     financial area of a construction company with generally
     the same duties but at a much higher level and considera-
     bly greater salary. You are greatly tempted even though
     you have been fairly happy in the insurance company.
     Should you take the better-paying, higher-level job?

16. One morning you wake up. Things have not been going
     well. You feel drained and at a dead end. And suddenly
     you realize what is wrong. It is your birthday and you
     are forty years old. Half your life is over. You haven't
     done any of the really important things you thought you
     would do. You have been working extremely hard with
     scarcely any vacation in two years. You and your wife
     are not getting along, are in fact on the edge of divorce,
     and this is the time, you suddenly feel, to chuck the
     whole show and try for the career you have always

dreamed of—a practice of your own, a new life in a new town. You have savings. You have done well financially. Mary, your wife, has been seeing someone else, and your son is going away to college, your daughter finishing high school. Should you take the plunge?

17. You have decided to take the plunge. You have decided to start your own practice in another town. You know where you want to live, but before that you will just take a vacation and bum around for a year. Then you will be refreshed and reoriented. Then you can start your practice. Should you take the year off? What do you need to do to start your new practice?

18. You have decided to take the plunge. You have always wanted to own your own business. You have a product you have developed and some ideas on marketing it, and you think you can make a success of it. What do you do first?

19. The die has been cast. You are cleaning out your office. You are going to another job in another company and you are sorting through your files. There is the stack of memos on the Alberra Program you initiated. It is obsolete now but in its day it was very successful. The first memo shows you initiated the project and outlines what you thought it could do. Then there are the engineering drawings—now obsolete but they could be useful in this new job. Here is the memo from Conroy praising the great job you did. Here is correspondence with some of your old associates in a personal vein, but these people may be useful to you in your new job. Here are the schematics you did for the Banion Project, and they can be very helpful in your new job. After all you made them. They are your schematics and the company never used them. They're probably no use now. Well, you'll dump a lot of this stuff, leave some and take the rest with you. What can you take with you?

20. You have decided to quit. You found something in another field and you are safe and you are finally free to get out of this hellhole. The job might have been possible if it weren't for that tyrant, Lanahan. He has made your life miserable long enough. Now revenge is sweet. You are going to let him know what you think of him. You are going to tell him to his face and you can't wait to see his expression. He has no idea you're leaving and he won't have you to kick around any more. You pack up the last of your things. And you walk across the office to his corner lair. You are going to let him have it. Is this a good idea?

PART V

□

LEGAL REMEDIES
—Key Court Cases that Show
What Has Been Decided on
Issues Affecting Jobholders

The job is so important to our society that there has grown up over a century a body of laws and regulations aimed at protecting a person under certain circumstances and in certain areas of his work life from discrimination or wrongful discharge.

These forms of protection have been of four general kinds: protecting the rights of those who wish to organize into unions and bargain collectively; protecting those seeking jobs or working in organizations against discrimination because of race, creed, color or sex; protecting those who may be wrongfully discharged for protesting or bringing to light illegal acts by the organization or acts or policies held to be against the public interest; and most recently, though by no means as clearly articulated as other forms of protection, an effort to obtain equity for the least protected of jobholders, the white-collar and middle-management group, by developing a trend toward sometimes modifying the so-called at-will discharge.

The at-will doctrine was based on the premise that an employer is free to discharge a worker at will, unless there is an express contractual agreement as to the duration of employment. The rule that employment for an indefinite term is terminable at will for any or no reason has historically been a

251

part of our free enterprise system and has been considered important to our economic welfare and growth. Absent any contractual agreement as to duration, the worker may leave the job at will and the organization may discharge the jobholder at will.

However, it has been recognized that there are situations where public policy and the public good demand that this doctrine be modified to some extent and that the jobholder be protected from what has come to be called abusive or wrongful discharge. Under the guidance of Alfred G. Feliu, a New York attorney specializing in employment relations, we outline briefly in this section examples of the four forms of legal protection and show some of the key cases that indicate the sort of protection courts have offered.

Mr. Feliu has identified the following key cases, which we summarize.

As our adviser has pointed out, however, legal remedies have a high cost in time, stress and money and should not be undertaken lightly. Mr. Feliu has noted, "Before deciding to pursue a legal remedy, a jobholder should be aware of the present realities of such action":

• It will probably take a number of years before the matter is finally resolved.

• He or she will probably have to pay 30 percent of whatever is recovered and perhaps an initial fee to the attorney.

• The stress of the contested litigation can take a heavy toll in the litigant and his or her family, and this may be the highest cost of all.

Nevertheless, as will be seen in these summarized court cases, the rights of a person with respect to his or her job are beginning to be recognized in ways that were not thought of a few decades ago or even a few years ago.

252

> *A single employee is helpless*
> *in dealing with an employer* . . .
>
> Chief Justice CHARLES EVANS HUGHES
> in U.S. Supreme Court decision up-
> holding the authority of the National
> Labor Relations Board to remedy un-
> fair labor practices

National Labor Relations Board *v*. Jones & Laughlin Steel Corporation

The year is 1937.

Ten union activists had been discharged from the Jones and Laughlin Steel Corporation. The corporation contended that it would not obey the National Labor Relations Board (NLRB) orders to reinstate them and that Congress had no right to regulate the relationship between labor and management.

The Supreme Court decision by a 5 to 4 vote upheld the authority of the NLRB to remedy unfair labor practices and in its ruling stated that "employees have as clear a right to organize and select their representation for lawful purposes as (management) has to organize its business and select its own officers and agents."

The corporation was ordered to reinstate the ten men with back pay and to post notices in the plants informing workers that it would not discriminate against union members.

> *Dismissal of an employee for refusing to violate a significant*
> *public policy as for example refusing to commit purjury is pro-*
> *hibited* . . .
>
> California District Court of Appeals

Petermann *v*. International Brotherhood

The year is 1959.

Peter Petermann, the business agent of Local 396 of the

Teamsters Union, had been subpoenaed by the California Assembly Internal Committee to testify at a hearing. The secretary-treasurer of the union instructed Petermann to make false and misleading statements to the committee at the hearing. Petermann did not follow these instructions. He answered all questions fully and truthfully. The day following the hearing, he was fired.

He sued.

The court faced a difficult legal precedent. The so-called at-will principle had always proved inviolate in the United States, so that, absent an express contractual agreement as to the duration of employment, an organization can dismiss an employee at will for any reason or for no reason. The court, with little to guide or rule its decision, found that "it would be obnoxious to the interests of the state and contrary to public policy and sound morality to allow an employer to discharge any employee, whether the employment be for a designated or an unspecified duration on the ground that the employee declined to commit purjury, a criminal offense . . ."

The court further noted that Petermann had been promised employment as long as his work was satisfactory and that, ironically the day before he delivered his testimony, the secretary-treasurer had commented to Petermann that his work was highly satisfactory.

In 1980 the California Supreme Court in a similar case extended broad protection against this type of discharge, thus vindicating Petermann's action.

If an employment practice which operates to exclude Negroes cannot be shown to be related to job performance, the practice is prohibited . . .

Griggs *v*. Duke Power Company

The year is 1971.

Willie S. Griggs, a black man, brought suit as representing a class of incumbent black employees at Duke Power Company, challenging as discriminatory the company's policy of requiring all new employees to have a high school degree and to pass a standardized aptitude test.

The company argued that since it required these qualifications from all employees, black and white, it could not be said to discriminate against any class. However, it was shown that blacks in greater proportion lacked these qualifications and that the qualifications were not necessarily related to job performance.

On September 25, 1972, a federal district court ordered that the Duke Power Company refrain from requiring that employees have a high school degree or pass a standardized intelligence test unless it can be shown that these requirements are related to satisfactory job performance.

That the employer intended to inflict emotional distress or should have known it would result, that the conduct was extreme and outrageous and utterly intolerable in a civilized community . . .

Findings of Supreme Judicial Court of Massachusetts

Agis *v.* Howard Johnson Company

The year is 1976.

The manager of this Howard Johnson restaurant called all the waitresses together. There was some stealing going on, he told them, and unless the responsible party came forward, he would begin firing the waitresses present, one by one, in alphabetical order. When no one admitted guilt, he began to carry out his threat, starting with Debra Agis.

Debra Agis sued.

By her own account, she testified, she was wretched following her dismissal. In addition to her lost wages and benefits, she suffered great mental anguish and distress at the injustice of that act and she attributed this mental anguish and distress directly to the manner of her dismissal. Her husband, James,

255

found that as a result of his wife's firing, he lost the full benefit of her companionship, her love, good company and attention and that their sexual relationship suffered as well.

Mrs. Agis sued the restaurant and the manager for "intentional or reckless affliction of emotional distress," and her husband sought recovery for loss of consortium, that is, the love, affection and companionship of his wife.

The court required four elements to recover: (1) that the employer intended to inflict emotional distress or should have known that it would result; (2) that the conduct was extreme and outrageous and utterly intolerable in a civilized community; (3) that the conduct pointed to caused the emotional distress; and (4) that the mental anguish was severe and beyond what reasonable people should be forced to endure.

The court found that these strict requirements were met in the case of Debra Agis and that her claims could be sustained. It also found that a spouse is entitled to recover for the injury suffered as a result of the outrageous conduct of this employer.

The absolute right to discharge at will an employee must be tempered by the further principle that where the employer's motivation for the discharge contravenes some substantial public policy, then the employer may be liable to the employee for damages . . .

West Virginia Supreme Court of Appeals

Harless v. First National Bank in Fairmont

The year is 1978.

John Harless, office manager of the consumer credit department of the First National Bank in Fairmont, came upon the fact that the bank was overcharging its customers on prepayment of their installment loans. He brought this illegal act to the attention of a supervisor, a vice-president, and later to a member of the board of directors.

He noticed soon after that bank files related to his claims began to be destroyed. He was demoted and his supervisor threatened him on several occasions. Later, however, the bank acknowledged the illegal practice and began to take corrective actions. Harless in turn was reinstated to his former position. However, when outside auditors arrived to review the records, Harless provided them with some of the customers' bank files that he had retrieved from the wastepaper basket. Soon after, he was fired.

Harless sued. The court looked to the state's Consumer Credit Protection Act, which gives consumers the right to sue for damages against violators of the law. It ruled that a clear and unequivocal public policy like protection against consumer fraud should not be frustrated by the discharge of an employee who seeks to ensure compliance with the law. The court found that a cause of action had been furnished by such a discharge even in the face of the previously inviolate at-will rule.

Harless was at first awarded $115,000 by a jury—$80,000 against the bank and $35,000 against the supervisor. This was reduced, first to $80,000 by the trial court and then four years later to $25,000 by the Supreme Court of Appeals.

> *Federal law is violated when a supervisor with the actual or constructive knowledge of the employer makes sexual advances or demands toward a subordinate employee and conditions that employee's job status, evaluation, continued employment, promotion or other aspects of career development on a favorable response to these advances or demands . . .*

Finding of the Federal Court of Appeals

Tomkins *v.* Public Electric & Gas Company

The year is 1977.

Adrienne Tomkins was invited to lunch by her new supervisor—to discuss her promotion, he said. Instead she spent the lunch hour fighting off his advances, both physical and verbal. In the most explicit language he told her that they could have a good working relationship only if she were to have sexual relations with him. His language was foul, and he attempted to use physical constraint to keep her. She finally broke away after he forcibly kissed her.

Her agitation was intense and she wanted to quit, but she could not afford to. She needed the job. She spoke to her supervisor's boss. He promised her a transfer to a comparable position within the company. Instead she was placed in an inferior, almost functionless job. Suddenly every department where she had worked began submitting reports to the personnel office, asserting that her performance in these jobs had been poor. Finally she was fired.

She went to the Equal Employment Opportunity Commission, but the agency refused to pursue her claim. She then went to federal court. She was told that sexual harassment and sexually motivated assault did not constitute sex discrimination under the law. In this finding the court asserted that federal laws against employment discrimination are not a remedy "for what amounts to physical attack motivated by sexual desire on the part of a supervisor and which happens to occur in a corporate corridor rather than a back alley."

The case was then appealed and at last Adrienne Tomkins's brave fight against this sexual tyranny was successful. The Federal Court of Appeals ruled that an employee is entitled to protection under federal law when sexual demands are made a term or condition of employment, that federal law is violated when a supervisor, with the actual or constructive knowledge of the employer, makes sexual advances or demands toward a subordinate employee and conditions that employee's job status, evaluation, continued employment, promotion or other aspects of career development on a favorable response to these advances or demands and that the employer must take prompt and appropriate remedial action after acquiring such knowledge.

The court ordered that Adrienne Tomkins be awarded $20,000 for her physical and emotional injury and $47,000 in court costs and attorney's fees. The company was ordered to notify all its nonunion employees of their rights under the employment discrimination laws, to establish a nonunion grievance committee or system and distribute a pamphlet detailing the grievance system's coverage. The company was ordered to present a film made by Adrienne Tomkins and her lawyer about job discrimination and, finally, the company was ordered to purge all adverse entries from Adrienne Tomkins's personnel file.

Adrienne Tomkins was finally vindicated, and sexual harassment was established as a violation of federal law.

> *The right of an employee to choose not to perform his assigned task because of a reasonable apprehension of death or serious injury coupled with a reasonable belief that no less drastic alternative is available . . .*
>
> U.S. Supreme Court

Whirlpool Corporation *v.* Marshall, Secretary of Labor

The year is 1980.

Virgil Deemer and Thomas Cornwall had refused to go out on the guard screen suspended above the plant floor one evening in 1974. Ten days before, a maintenance man had fallen to his death through an older section of the screen. Deemer and Cornwall had the day before spoken about dangerous areas in the screen to both the plant safety director and the Occupation Safety and Health Administration (OSHA). The men were sent home that evening, docked a night's pay and given an official reprimand.

The Secretary of Labor had issued regulations protecting employees in this type of situation, that is, in a situation where a worker reasonably believes that an assigned task may present an imminent risk of death or serious injury and there is insufficient time to apprise the employer or OSHA of the danger. In coming to the defense of Deemer and Cornwall in this instance, however, the Secretary of Labor was adjudged as having exceeded his authority in enacting the regulation by a federal court of appeals. The case was brought before the Supreme Court.

The Court first considered the preamble of the Occupational Safety and Health Act, which had been enacted by Congress. The preamble stated as its goal "to assure so far as possible every working man and woman in the Nation safe and healthful working conditions and to preserve our human resources." The Secretary was given broad authority to fashion regulations that serve these purposes.

The Court stated: "The Act does not wait for an employee to die or become injured. It authorizes the promulgation of health and safety standards and the issuance of citations in the hope that these will prevent deaths or injuries from ever occurring. It would seem anomalous to construe an act so directed and constructed as prohibiting an employee, with no other reasonable alternative, the freedom to withdraw from a workplace environment that he reasonably believes is highly dangerous." The Court concluded that the Secretary had acted within his authority and upheld the regulation.

Deemer and Cornwall, six years after the event, were given their night's pay back and had all references to the disciplinary suspension and reprimand expunged from their personnel files.

To allow an employer to avoid the vesting of rights in a pension plan after thirteen years of service by a model employee under the guise of the employment at will doctrine does not sit well with this court . . .

U.S. District Court, New York

Savodnik *v.* Korvettes, Inc.

The year is 1980.

Morton Savodnik had put in thirteen years of faithful service to the company. He had been a model employee, received frequent promotions and annual raises, and he looked forward to receiving his pension soon under the company pension plan.

Then one day not long before his pension was about to be vested, he was summarily dismissed. He claimed that the reason he was fired was that his pension was about to be vested. The company did not deny this. The company instead contended that even if that were the reason, it had every right to dismiss Savodnik for any reason or for no reason, since no term of employment of a definite duration had been made. The company made the point that an at-will employee could under the law be fired for even a bad reason.

Savodnik sued.

The federal court trying the case acknowledged that in that state the company had accurately described the law. Nevertheless, the court focused on the strong public policy in favor of protecting the integrity of pension plans and held that the company's actions suggested an unwillingness to carry out its obligations under the law and that an attempt to avoid these obligations by systematically terminating its employees just prior to the vesting of their pensions could not be tolerated. The court concluded that New York courts would undoubtedly view Savodnik's dismissal as "abusive discharge." The court acknowledged that this might constitute a modification of the at-will doctrine but quoted a classic article written by Oliver Wendell Holmes, Jr.: "It is revolting to have no better reason for a rule of law," Holmes had written, "than that it was laid down in the time of Henry IV. It is still more revolting if the grounds upon which it was laid down have vanished long since, and the rule simply persists from blind imitation of the past."

Morton Savodnik was reinstated.

The Age Discrimination in Employment Act makes it unlawful for an employer to discharge any individual because of such individual's age . . .

U.S. Court of Appeals

Cancellier *v.* Federated Department Stores

The year is 1982.

Phillip Cancellier, a vice-president of stores and operations of I. Magnin Company, had been with the firm for twenty-five years. John Costello, a divisional merchandise manager for accessories, had been with the company for seventeen years and Zelora Smith Ritter, a buyer of sportswear, had been with I. Magnin eighteen years.

In early 1978, as part of a general reorganization of the company, these three long-service employees, all over forty, were dismissed. It was averred that new blood was needed. The company brought in younger people for these posts. The three former executives then sued under the federal Age Discrimination in Employment Act and under a California law for breach of an implied covenant of good faith and fair dealing.

Under the Age Discrimination in Employment Act, workers between the ages of forty and seventy may not be discriminated against on the basis of their age. Decisions affecting jobholders over forty years old must be rooted in job-related concerns, for example, ability to perform assigned tasks, and not on considerations of age.

In this case the evidence seemed to the jury to show clearly that these executives were dismissed purely because of age rather than any inability to perform their assigned tasks. The result was the return of one of the largest jury awards of its kind. The jury upheld the executives' claims under both theories. They awarded Phillip Cancellier $800,000, John Costello, $600,000, and Zelora Smith Ritter, $500,000.

The court cases summarized in this part are key cases that show the changing social views and the increasing efforts by society to protect us in our jobs. There have been many other cases and there are new cases arising affecting jobs and reflecting this trend toward increased protection of jobholders, protection from discrimination by reason of race, color, creed, sex or age, against gross injustice and wrongful discharge.

Legal remedies, however, because of the cost in time and money and the tremendous emotional trauma, are always essentially a last resort and one undertaken only where the recovery may be substantial and the principle very great and worth the great sacrifice demanded.

PART VI

□

ANSWERS AND REFERENCES TO SELF-ASSESSMENT QUESTIONNAIRES

ANSWERS AND REFERENCES TO
SELF-ASSESSMENT QUESTIONNAIRES

The suggested answers to these Self-assessment Questionnaires lie mostly in the principles, techniques and tactics outlined in the vignettes and sections referred to, but they can only be suggestive, since the realities of your own situation in each case must determine the best strategy. While the principles offered are sound, our advisers felt that in many cases there were so many variables possible in the situation that only the jobholder who experienced the situation could give a valid response. Nevertheless, we have answered the questions based on the principles, tactics and strategies outlined in the references.

Answers to Part II Self-assessment on the Work

1. The common measures of competence are indicated in "Are you competent?" page 24. You must find out specifically what measures of competence you are being judged by from your boss or other authority who sets such standards. If none have been set, study the job and set your own.

2. Your functional skills may consist of anything from typing to programming a computer. Look at the two that are most useful in your job. Managerial skills are indicated in the list on page

31 under "Skills." They range from designing plans to leading a meeting.

3. There are twelve time wasters listed under "Reasonable Hours and Time Management," page 34, from lack of planning to inability to make decisions. Think of those habits that fall into the time-wasting categories and consider which remedies might work for you.

4. Every job has a measure of efficiency, which is usually based on the measure of competence in the job: number of tasks performed per day or the like. If no measure of efficiency has been established on your job, it would be advantageous for you to establish one yourself. You will then know when you have done a good day's work. See "Being Efficient."

5. The measure of effectiveness on a job depends on factors outside of the job itself. You must ask yourself what results that are profitable to the whole organization and its purposes are desirable in your job. Efficiency is not enough. One can be efficient in losing profit, if the job's reason for being is not kept in mind. See "Being Effective."

6. If your answer is often, you know you are in trouble. Whether this is through lack of planning, lack of working out a compromise between your work and your home or a lack of respect for your work and your homelife, you may be endangering a good job. See "Bringing the Home into the Office."

7. Again if your answer is often, you must consider whether you are showing your family the respect and consideration they deserve. You may go through periods in establishing yourself, particularly in professions, when the work overwhelms the family and its life. Many divorces and neglected children are the result of the person who allows his or her work to overwhelm personal life.

8. If you find you have missed an unusual number of vacations or holidays because of work, you should look at certain other aspects of your work life. Becoming a workaholic is a serious matter. See "Killing Yourself."

9. The inability to function at times may be a symptom of a seri-

ous difficulty in your life or it may be simply the normal ennui that overcomes us all at times. See "Goofing Off."

10. You may notice that the most common characteristics of unusually productive workers are that they are able to plan and to delegate. Keeping "the list" and knowing who can do what well with the ability to persuade have given many a manager the strength of ten. See "Who's the Best Worker?"

11. Look at your own job carefully. Select those aspects of the job that can be quantified. Put numbers on them. They may reveal things about your work to you that will surprise you and that you can turn to advantage. See "Measuring Yourself."

12. Do you know from what sources most anxiety springs? Have you come to terms with the dependency factor? See "Anxiety." You must work out your own remedy, based on your own personality and situation. No one is without periods of anxiety from the sense of panic at four in the morning because of unpaid bills to the depressions from imagined catastrophes. Job-related anxieties can be mitigated by understanding them and sometimes bringing them into the open.

13. Work should be exhilarating. It should be fun. If you have identified what it is you really like to do, structure your job to get the most pleasure, the most fun from it. Emphasize those parts of the job that give you the most pleasure. On some days you should find you can't wait to get in in the morning and you hate to leave at night. See "Loving the Work."

14. Every job has scutwork, has some drudgery to it. Learn to do this cheerfully and fast. If possible, find out what parts of your job others like that you hate and see whether you can delegate. You cannot get rid of all the bad parts of your job but you need not emphasize them and you can learn to handle them quickly to get them out of the way. See "Hating the Work."

15. We are all bored sometimes just as we are all boring sometimes, but chronic boredom is a symptom of something more serious. It should be looked at carefully. See "Boredom."

16. At some time in your life, you may be offered a transfer. At some time in your work life, you may face a situation where

you have to accept a transfer to keep your job or to go further in your career. For example, if an organization moves its headquarters to another city, you may have no choice but to go with them or to find another job. Nevertheless, there are seven considerations you need address in making any decision. See "Getting Transferred."

17. Did you make a mistake in going in to see your boss to get transferred to marketing? The answer is no. You were right, regardless of his reaction. It is important to you and to the organization that you broaden your experience and the scope of your abilities. Your boss may not be able to give you such a transfer immediately or may be unwilling to let you go, but it is important that the boss know your plans and desires and that others in authority know them, if you are to get ahead.

18. Should you keep up the good work and be patient? Keep up the good work by all means but do not be patient. Set up a reasonable career path and work out where you should be now. No one is going to give it to you. You must know what you want to do and where you want to be and take immediate steps to get there. These steps may require looking around the organization and perhaps asking for a transfer to some other area, if no promotion is offered, or in extreme cases turning your attention to the outside work world to find the place you want to be at that period. See "Career."

Part III, Suggested Answers to Part III Questionnaire with References

1. The purpose of describing your relationship with your boss is to bring to your attention the fact that you may not know enough about his or her problems, way of thinking, style or goals. If you understand these things, you will be able to deal with your boss profitably for you both. The boss's job should be of great concern to you, just as your job is to the boss. Your relationship with your boss is of great importance not just to both but to the organization as well. See "The World According to the Boss" and "Managing Up."

2. Here again you are asked to look at your boss but also at the organization of which you both are a part. Look at his standing in that organization. Has your boss plateaued out? Is he or she a comer? What is your boss's reputation? How does your boss fit into the organization as a whole? See "The World According to the Company," "Supervisory Styles," "The Killer Boss."

3. You must understand how conflicting goals, desires and pressures often turn otherwise decent people into manipulators, politicians, troublemakers and sometimes career killers. You must learn what tactics and stratagems are used and how to counter them from withholding essential information, downgrading you to your superior or using various methods of sabotaging a project. Here are some possible responses to the specific situations presented:

• You are embarrassed at a meeting because you were not sent the right figures or information. Turn to the perpetrator in front of those at the meeting and say something like, "Jim, I guess you forgot to send me the latest figures and I relied on your earlier ones. Now please tell me and the group what the facts actually are. Next time I'm sure I'll be given the right information."

• Keep a copy of your original memorandum. From then on send copies of any memoranda on new ideas or other matters to others in the organization. Depending on whether it will be to your benefit to warn this person, send him a little note thanking him for using your original idea with a copy of your original memorandum attached. Also consider getting a transfer. Your career could be stymied by this type of man. See "The Killer Boss."

• Find an occasion to see your boss. Mention that Clem has been telling people that you were responsible for the Blow-Up Project. Mention you had nothing to do with it but that it might have been one of those projects no one could have saved. See "He's Out to Get Me."

• You find you cannot get through the bureaucracy on a project. Find out why they are stonewalling you, what it is that they think may happen if the project goes through. Usually there is a motive behind such sabotage and if you can identify it, you may be able to allay fears and get cooperation. Brute force will do no good. Bureaucracies can eat up the strongest manager. You must find what will motivate them to get your project through. See "He's Out to Get Me," "The Grapevine," "Persuading."

• It is possible that the "kind friend" is simply a troublemaker. It is possible that someone is out to get you and that your friend is really a kind friend, in which case find out why this person is out to get you and what methods he or she intends to use. It is possible that, as your friend tells you, someone does not like you. Not everyone in the world is going to like us, unfortunately. See "Troublemaker" and "Why Doesn't He/She Like Me?"

4. If you need to get something done fast, the fastest form of communicating is personal communication. Always go in person. Avoid formal channels. The person who operates only through formal channels rarely gets anything done fast. There are times, of course, when formal channels are necessary, but those who have learned to operate in the great sea of informal communicating will be most able to get things done. It is fine to be able to write a good memo or a splendid report or a letter but it is even more important in communicating to be able to get out there in person and to know how to talk to and handle people. See "Communicating."

5. The purpose of looking at how people in your organization deal with those reporting to them is to give yourself some insight as to the culture of the organization. Is your organization somewhat authoritarian? If so, it tends to reward people who like to use their authority and it hires people who are comfortable in an authoritarian atmosphere. If it is a permissive structure and people operate best in a looser structure, a more informal structure, then this is a clue to you as to how you should deal with your superiors and those reporting to you as well as your associates. While you will probably understand this subconsciously and adapt yourself, it is a good idea to have

consciously examined this as well as other aspects of the organization's culture. You will then be able to plan your approaches to get things done. See "Supervisory Styles," "Do You Know the Language?" and "The World According to the Company."

6. Most people think they listen pretty well. Most people think they can listen well when they want to, but the truth is most of us listen very badly and few of us have any idea of what listening entails. We tend to fail at all four areas of listening—at the level of hearing, of interpreting, of evaluating and of responding. There are eighty-two techniques, tactics and strategies that may make you a better listener—from establishing an agreeable atmosphere to summarizing the substance of what you have heard to the speaker to taking notes where possible. These eighty-two tactics can help you. See "Listening." Then listen. You will become popular. Furthermore, the higher you go in your career, the more you will have to listen. Someone has said that 80 percent of a top executive's job is listening and another 9 percent is keeping his mouth shut.

7. There is one rule to speaking frankly, particularly if your frankness will offend or disturb the recipient. That rule or principle to guide you is: What good will it do? If speaking frankly to your superior will do some good, get something done, then do so, even at the cost of some unpleasantness for yourself. If it will only relieve your feelings, forget it. The same is true in speaking frankly to someone reporting to you. If it will do some good, if it will gain something, get something done, then do it. If you can simply relieve your feelings or take pride in your outspokenness, it is generally not worth it. Observe business manners, observe the ceremonies. Good manners are a splendid asset, an asset to you, a pleasure to all those who deal with you.

8. Like the rule on speaking frankly, so the rule on passing along a rumor about someone you dislike: What good will it do? If it will do some good, forewarn someone, prevent some mischief, pass it on. If it will only relieve your own feelings or assuage your dislike, forget it.

273

9. Once again, being a loner is not a crime. It is possible that your job relationships will suffer to some degree. People sometimes resent loners, feel they are unfriendly. That is their problem, not yours. Yours is to do your work as best you can, to be courteous and go your own way. As Christopher Morley said, "There is only one success: to be able to spend your life in your own way."

10. Should you send that strong memo that will point out a major deficiency in the division's operations? The answer is no. Any memo you send should offer values, not criticism. Send a memo by all means, but work out what advantage your change of procedure will gain for the recipient and the division and then tell how he or she and the division can get that advantage by making this or that change. Criticisms, no matter how constructive, rarely do much good. They are received reluctantly (except by masochists) and often not acted upon, and worst of all the sender may be perceived as a troublemaker who should be minding his own business.

11. In any presentation in which you are trying to persuade others to do something, your first considerations should be: (1) What effect will what you are asking have on those you are trying to persuade? (2) What values or benefits will the recipients of your message gain by your proposal? and (3) Can you structure your presentation so that you lead off with these values and conclude with these benefits?

12. You look around in the organization for a job you can do well in some other department or group, find out whether there is any possibility of breaking in there and then ask specifically for a transfer to that area in order to broaden your experience and usefulness to the organization. It is useless and probably counterproductive to let the killer boss suspect that he or she is what you are trying to get away from. Nevertheless, it is important that you get away, either through a transfer or turning to the outside in finding another job. See "The Killer Boss."

13. It is usually not fatal to be disliked by one or two people. To be disliked by everybody is another matter and one to be taken

seriously. We suggest nine possibilities you may want to consider. See "Why Doesn't He/She Like Me?"

14. There is no easy one way to meet this problem. You must see to it that the truth about the misleading rumor is brought to the attention of those who count in your job, if possible through a memorandum setting the matter straight, if not through personally approaching those who would be misled by the rumor. You can begin by saying, "I understand there is a rumor that . . ." and end by saying, "I just wanted you to know that . . ." or "I didn't want you to think that . . ."

15. Those who are most successful in negotiating the heights in an organization have a mentor, someone of importance who cares for them, likes them and wants to see them come along. The best way to find a mentor is to approach the opinion leaders in an organization and in your field and get to know them. You approach them by touching on projects in which they are particularly interested, and if your interest in these projects or these fields is genuine and you seek their help, you will usually arouse their interest in you and your work and career. Opinion leaders are more sensitive, responsive and busier than others, so your approach must include something significant to them. Eventually one or another of them may become your mentor and take an interest in you and your career. See "Mentor."

16. Everyone seems to tell you not to listen to gossip and rumor. Don't you believe it. If you are not in the flow of gossip and rumor, you will not know what is going on. That is where the action is. To plug into the grapevine and learn what is going on, you need first to get out of your office and into the field, talk to a lot of people, show an interest in events and rumors, offer up relevant information yourself, become trusted and keep up your outside contacts. These contacts must be informal and on a human level. You come out like a human being who would like to be part of the organization's world. See "The Grapevine."

17. You cannot understand what someone is really saying until you

understand the person. Words don't have meaning; people have meaning—as the linguists tell us. If you are not sure what your boss means when telling you something, ask the boss's secretary or friend what is really meant. Then ask how it would be best for you to respond. See "What Does He Really Want?" and "Do You Know the Language?"

18. You should get to know opinion leaders in an organization. The trick is to find out who they are. They can be in any part of the organization and at any level. A warehouse foreman can be an opinion leader as well as a vice-chairman. A secretary can be an opinion leader as well as her boss's boss. Usually someone bright in Personnel or Human Resources, if you get to know them, can tell you who swings weight in the organization. These are the opinion leaders. It will pay you to get to know them if you want to get a project through or know what is going on of significance in the company. See "Opinion Leaders."

19. Being loyal simply means caring. If you care about the organization and its values, people and reputation, you are more than likely loyal, whether you agree with all its policies or not. See "Loyalty."

20. The first thing to do in a low-morale group is not to join in the general griping and despair. It is more important to be optimistic and upbeat in a low-morale situation than in a high-morale group. Morale can be destroyed in many ways and for many reasons, and in such cases only courage and optimism can save the group from dissolution. See "Morale."

21. You do not have to put up with sexual harassment, but for your own sake it is best to handle the situation with as much tact and common sense as you can. We suggest an approach and five steps you can take, depending on your situation. See "Sexual Harassment" and the case in Part V, "Tomkins v. Public Electric and Gas Company."

22. Usually your job is not endangered by your having an affair with an associate, if it is kept discreet. Organizations are loath to become involved in personal matters of this sort. The cases

of affairs in which the job (usually the woman's) was endangered arose from a belief that there was a conflict of interest in the promotion or privileges of one of the parties through the support of the other. See "Office Romance."

23. Successful women cited "lack of confidence" as the greatest obstacle they had faced in their careers. Others mentioned limited education, inability to break into the Old Boy network and other support networks that exist in male-dominated organizations. Many cited the tremendous strain between their work life and their homelife, a strain even greater than that faced by most men. And finally, despite the enormous strides women have made in the last decade and even though women now constitute half the work force, the role of women in the work world is generally less secure and less rewarding than that of men. Our society is still male-oriented and male-dominated. See "If You Are a Woman."

24. Learning to take charge comes largely through experience. However, if you have learned what managing means and how to get along with people, you have all the tools to handle any assignment within your competence. Your problem will be to use them. See " 'I'm Running This' " and "Power."

25. If you are human, these moments will occur, and particularly if you care about what you are doing and about your work. Avoid, if you can, getting a reputation for being temperamental and hard to deal with. What could ruin your career more than the occasional blowup is the shutting off of contacts, if people become afraid of offending you. Information dries up, essential human contacts are lost and you isolate yourself if you become known as temperamental.

26. Once again, you must know your boss, not just what is being said. You must be able to interpret what is really wanted, not necessarily what the person says is wanted. You must listen intelligently. If you are not sure what your boss is really saying, ask someone who knows the boss well. See "What Does He Really Want?"

27. You have three main sources of power available to you in

varying degrees: the power of your position, that is the authority your formal position gives you as defined in the job description, your personality, the ability to influence people through
your friendliness, persuasive ability and the feelings of affection or liking people important to the project may have for you
and the importance or contribution of the project itself. There
are other sources of power available also—the number of favors you have done others and your reputation, which is a
factor of your own former contributions to the organization
and to others. And finally there is a well of power in knowing
who are the opinion leaders and getting them on your side in
putting over the project. See "Power."

28. One of the most difficult adjustments you must make as you go
up in your career is leaving behind some of your old gang and
some of your old habits. In this case you are no longer "one of
the gang," and you should no longer go to the Friday-night
beer busts. You must face up to the fact that you may be
perceived as snobbish or as having had the promotion go to
your head. This is a fact of life, part of the price the new job
imposes on you if you are to fulfill it effectively. See "New
Position."

29. Whenever you come to a turning point in your life or your
career, a promotion, an age-related crisis, a major change of
any sort, it is a good idea to turn and look at your career once
more. Those who succeed best map their careers. They do not
leave everything to chance and the fates. Mapping a career or
looking once more at your career requires two major steps.
The first is a self-analysis. You look at your résumé or you
make up a new one to see what you look like from a somewhat
objective viewpoint. Secondly, you turn your attention to your
dreams. Where do you want to go? Where do you want to be?
You then write these dreams and goals down. First, you write
out your short-range goals on the job, what you hope to accomplish this year and next. Second, you write out as best you can
the longer-range goals—where you want to be five or ten years
from now. Third, you consider your life-style and the way your
family or those for whom you are responsible would like to

live, and finally you try to map out the things you will have to do from now on to meet these goals, to make these dreams come true. Thinking about your job and life at midnight is one thing. Doing something about it is another. See "Career."

Suggested Answers to Part IV Questionnaires with References

1. The time has come, particularly if you have been immersed in a demanding job, to lift your head and look around you. If the job has been very demanding and very interesting, it is likely that you have lost contact with what is going on outside. As the job comes to an end, you must try to reorient yourself, to look around, to see what has been going on in the outside job world. You must ask yourself the old questions: Do I know what is going on in my field outside my organization? Have I kept any contacts with others of similar interests and expertise outside the organization? How long has it been since I had lunch with someone in my network of contacts? See "Looking Around."

2. Now is the time also to see where the experience you have gained puts you in relation to the outside market. Have you been looking at what is going on in your field, what part your field plays in the economy and in market demand? Have there been promotions among your friends, raises in salary? What are you worth now in the market place? It is time to get out and find out. See "Sizing Up the Market" and "Are You Being Paid What You're Worth?"

3. You must now reassess your prospects in that organization. You might ask your boss to be a bit more explicit as to your prospects in the company, when he thinks you will be ready for a promotion and a raise, what he would do in your place. Meanwhile, you should be exploring the possibilities in the marketplace and talking with your mentor and your friends. You should not at any time make threats to your boss, such as: "If you can't do anything for me, I will have to make other plans," or "I'll have to start looking around." Just look into your options and be quiet about it. Patience is a relative term

and, while you may seem patient and passive, you should not be so. Your career and value are too important. See "When to Go," "When to Stay."

4. You have got to sit down and look at yourself. You have got to ask yourself some searching questions: Why did you leave the last job? Why did you leave the job before? What is it in your makeup or situation that causes you to jump from one job to another, that makes it difficult for you to serve your time apprenticeships, to settle down and try to go the distance? You must try to be honest with yourself. Work up a résumé and look at the way it must seem to a personnel director when you jump from one job to another over a period of from six months to a year during the last few years. No, it would be better for you to try to give at least one job a few years before you jump to the next. See "Jumping."

5. Every career has setbacks, and these should be evaluated objectively. Even though you have been passed over for a promotion, are your overall prospects still pretty good? How is your standing in the organization? Whether you should leave the present job and take the equal job in another organization will depend on your assessment of your overall prospects, not on this possibly temporary setback. If you move to another organization, you have to start all over to build your reputation and standing. You must weight the cost of starting over with the cost of living through the setback. That will tell you whether you should accept the new offer. See "When to Stay."

6. One of the first things you can do, when you have come to a crossroads and feel unsure of your destination and of what you have accomplished, is to work up or redo a résumé. The résumé will give you a picture of what you have accomplished and where you seem to be now. See "Your résumé."

7. John Wareham, the international executive recruiter, suggested that you answer, "I will be glad to help you but may I call you back?" This will give you a chance to check out the reputation of the executive recruiting firm and to be sure it is bona fide. Then call back and listen to what is offered. See "Executive Recruiters."

280

8. First, you should check your organization's policy on taking other jobs. Most organizations have a restriction on taking another job, moonlighting where there may be a conflict of interest. If there is a general restriction on taking any other job, you might go in to see your boss and, if there is no conflict, ask for an exception. See "Moonlighting."

9. Even if you are satisfied, go over and talk to your friend. You lose nothing by checking out such vague offers. However, it is important not to be deluded into thinking you have a firm offer or relying too much on such a possibility at a future time. Organizations sometimes have immediate needs when you are golden, but these needs may evaporate at any time in the future. See "Being Romanced."

10. You must ask yourself whether you have stayed too long. You must ask yourself if you have married the organization for better or worse, and consider whether the worse may not be permanent. If you have reached your capacity level and feel comfortable and content in your job, it is not a crime to progress no further. This may be where you really want to be in terms of your overall career and life. If so, fine. If not, you have stayed too long. You should start looking around. See "When to Go."

11. Here again, consider whether this new tyrant placed over you is a temporary or permanent setback. Does it look as if he would last? Does it look as if his abrasive and tyrannical personality may not quickly bring about his downfall? The same objective evaluation of this setback should obtain as that in which you have been passed over for a promotion. How serious is this setback in terms of your overall career? How will it affect your health and outlook on the world? If it is serious, if it will affect your health and emotional stability, then by all means waste no time in trying to place yourself elsewhere. First try to get a transfer. Then and at the same time look around outside the organization. See "When to Stay," "When to Go."

12. Keep it quiet. You have others to talk over your decision to make the move with—your family, outside friends, perhaps your mentor. Do not go in and tell the boss or the company

about it until the commitment has been made and it is irrevocable. See "Keeping It Quiet."

13. You are faced with a truly wrenching dilemma. A transfer and a promotion, no matter how valuable to you and your career, must be assessed also in terms of its affect on your spouse and children. In the old days, where the man went, there the family went; what the man's career demanded, the family must accede to. No longer. A number of marriages have foundered on the conflict between the husband's and wife's careers. The decision must be one arrived at with the whole family and in this particular instance must be worked out in some way to take into account the wife's business and career. See "Getting Transferred" and "Talking It over with the Family."

14. This is the dilemma of the counteroffer, the bane of most executive recruiters' lives. If you have decided to take the new offer, you should already have discounted what your own organization can do for you. You should have first explored the matter and not be lured by the boss's new interest in keeping you. If you have really arrived at the decision to move, the problems that were with you with your old organization will probably remain even with the new promotion offered. It is rare that you will remain satisfied if you take the counteroffer. See "The Counteroffer."

15. You have been working in an old-line insurance company. Should you take the better-paying, higher-level job in a big construction company? The duties are the same. You must take into consideration that you will be moving from one kind of corporate culture to another and assess whether you can live in such a different culture. The insurance company has a *process* culture where you concentrate on how the job should be done since it is hard to measure what it is you do. The construction company generally has a *tough-guy macho* culture characterized by high risks and quick feedback. Can you work in that atmosphere? See "Corporate Cultures."

16. You have obviously come to a crossroads in your life and in your career. You are probably suffering one of the three major age crises most people go through—this one the midlife crisis,

described in so many books such as Gail Sheehy's *Passages*. This is a particularly dangerous time to take plunges. What is important now is to consider every step you take very carefully and as objectively as possible. Have you done some career planning that really takes into account where you want to be five and ten years from now? You should take the plunge not to escape a difficult part of your life but to move your life and career toward something you really want. If you are not sure what you want, sit tight. If you really know what you want and have planned for it, take the plunge. See "Age."

17. Do you really want to leave your organization for a practice of your own? Have you considered all the factors involved in setting up a successful practice? Have you asked yourself the four basic questions in going into your own practice? Are you ready? If not, take your time. Do not take the year off at this time. Keep your old job until you are ready to make the move to your own practice. If you are moving to another town to start your life over, you need to spend some time studying the potential of your own practice in that town. See "Becoming a Consultant."

18. Once more, if you have come to a careful decision about your life and want a business of your own, you must do some planning and studying for it. You must understand the risks and have the stamina and the willingness to take them. You must understand the costs in time and emotional turmoil. The first thing you do, if you have then come to a decision to take the plunge, is to formulate a business plan with its nine fundamental elements. See "Going into Business for Yourself."

19. The company owns a lot of things you have done. You cannot take with you the Alberra Program, except the memo showing you initiated it. You cannot take the engineering drawings or the schematics you did for the Banion Project. You can take correspondence with some of your old associates. You can take the memorandum from Conroy praising you for the great job you did and you can take your memories and experience. See "What You Can Take with You and What You Can't."

20. What pleasure it would be to allow yourself the luxury of tell-

ing Lanahan what you think of him. How you will savor it later and go over every look of surprise, incredulity and anger on his face. How delightful it will be to recount to your wife and your friends what you said and what he said and how it all ended in a big fat explosion. Don't do it. Deprive yourself of that pleasure. It is useless. It is a bad idea. It will do nobody any good. If, however, a calm memo on why you are leaving may help some of the other poor victims of this person's vindictiveness and tyranny, send such a memo, written calmly and in a quiet tone, to Personnel and to Lanahan's superior. Otherwise, forget it. Leave right. See "Leaving Right."

□

ENVOI

Social trends, custom and present environment are on the side of the jobholder. The work ethic is still paramount in this society. We noted at the beginning that almost all of us from the janitor to the chairman of the board are jobholders, that entrepreneurs, professional people and practitioners approach their work as jobs in the same way and all consider this work as their most valuable single asset.

Our jobs are generally the main source of our livelihood—and the most absorbing and demanding of all our life's activities. We spend most of our time on our jobs. We build our futures on them, our marriages, our hopes of supporting and educating our children and to a degree our status, our sense of our own self-worth. Love and work are the two mainsprings of human life on which we bestow supreme values and which cannot be fulfilled for us except through others. Through these areas we gain our knowledge of ourselves and of the world. Through them we live a full life.

If this book has in some small measure made a contribution to your understanding and enjoyment of your life in the work world, it will have amply fulfilled its purpose.

□

SUGGESTED READING

There are literally hundreds of books on work and the work world. Those selected here seem to the author the most helpful, witty or full of insight of the vast literature. Some of them are classics; others are not so well known. All the books quoted in this handbook are listed also.

Best, Fred: *Flexible Life Scheduling,* Praeger Publishers, New York 1980.

Bolles, Richard Nelson: *What Color Is Your Parachute,* Ten Speed Press, Berkeley, Calif., 1982.

Butler, Robert E., and Donald Rappaport: *Money & Your Business—How to Get It, How to Manage It, How to Keep It,* New York Institute of Finance, 70 Pine Street, New York, NY 10005.

Creedy, Richard E.: *Guide to Successful Self-Employment.* Creedy Associates, New York.

DeBono, Edward: *Opportunities: A Handbook of Business Opportunity,* Penguin, New York, 1981.

de Mare, George: *Communicating at the Top,* John Wiley & Sons, New York, 1979.

———— (with Joanne Summerfield): *Corporate Lives,* VanNostrand Reinhold, New York, 1976.

———— (co-author): *Listening—It Can Change Your Life,* John Wiley & Sons, New York, 1983.

Dowling, Colette: *The Cinderella Complex,* Pocket Books, New York, 1981.

Drucker, Peter: *Managing,* Harper & Row, New York, 1978.

Ewing, David W.: *Do It My Way or You're Fired,* John Wiley & Sons, New York, 1983

Gracian, Balthasar: *The Art of Worldly Wisdom,* Fredrick Ungar, New York, 1967.

Hersberg, Frederick: *Work and the Nature of Man,* New American Library, New York, 1973.

Kaplan, Glenn: *The Big Time—How Success Really Works in 14 Top Business Careers,* Congdon & Weeds, New York, 1981.

McCarthy, John J.: *Why Managers Fail,* McGraw-Hill, New York, 1978.

Maccoby, Michael: *The Gamesman,* Simon & Schuster, New York, 1976.

Mackenzie, Alec R.: *The Time Trap,* McGraw-Hill, New York, 1975.

Naisbitt, John: *Megatrends,* Warner Books, New York, 1982.

Ogilvie, David: *Confessions of an Advertising Man,* Atheneum, New York, 1963.

Peter, Laurence F., and Raymond Hull: *The Peter Principle,* William Morrow, New York, 1969.

Rohrlich, J. B., M.D.: *Work and Love,* Summit Books, New York, 1978.

Schrank, Robert: *10,000 Working Days,* MIT Press, Cambridge, Mass., 1978.

Sheehy, Gail: *Pathfinders,* William Morrow, New York, 1981.

————: *Passages,* Bantam, New York, 1977.

Steil, Lyman K.: *Listening—It Can Change Your Life,* John Wiley & Sons, New York, 1983.

Summerfield, Joanne: *Corporate Lives,* VanNostrand Reinhold, New York, 1976.

————: *Listening—It Can Change Your Life,* John Wiley & Sons, New York, 1983.

Terkel, Studs: *Working,* Avon Books, New York, 1978.

Townsend, Robert: *Up the Organization,* Knopf, New York, 1970.

Wareham, John: *Secrets of a Corporate Headhunter,* TEI Books, New York, 1980.

INDEX

293

297